MW01531936

LUIGI FLEISCHMANN

FROM FIUME TO NAVELLI
A Sixteen-Year-Old's Narrative of the Fleischmann
Family and Other Free Internees in Fascist Italy
September 1943–June 1944

LUIGI FLEISCHMANN

FROM FIUME
TO NAVELLI

A Sixteen-Year-Old's Narrative
of the Fleischmann Family
and Other Free Internees in Fascist Italy
September 1943–June 1944

Yad Vashem • Jerusalem • 2007

Luigi Fleischmann
From Fiume to Navelli
A Sixteen-Year-Old's Narrative of the Fleischmann Family
and Other Free Internees in Fascist Italy
September 1943–June 1944

Translated by Luigi Fleischmann from the Italian:
Un Ragazzo Ebreo Nelle Retrovie

Many thanks to Daniella Ashkenazy for her aid and assistance.

Managing Editor: Daniella Zaidman-Mauer
Language Editor: Leah Goldstein

ISBN 978-965-308-297-7
Danacode 268-477

© 2007 Yad Vashem
P.O.B. 3477, Jerusalem 91034
e-mail: publications.marketing@yadvashem.org.il

All rights of the English edition are reserved
to Yad Vashem

Responsibility for the opinions expressed in this publication
is solely that of the author.

All rights reserved. This book may not be reproduced, in whole or
part, in any form, without written permission from the publisher.

Typesetting: Judith Sternberg
Produced by Offset Nathan Shlomo Press

Printed in Jerusalem, Israel

To Noga, who believed in the diary and strived for years to convey it to the world. To my daughters, Liora and Elisheva, who drank in their father's stories from the war with great thirst — especially Liora, who tirelessly typed each page as I told her my story, slowly turning the diary into reality.

This book is also dedicated to the people of Navelli, who displayed the ultimate human kindness by taking in and often saving the lives of the people mentioned here.

Table of Contents

Prologue

Many years have passed since the following pages were written in the original Italian. Because of this, I feel it is necessary to explain and clarify facts that may be unfamiliar to the reader today — facts regarding the situation of the Jews in Italy in the period prior to the outbreak of the Second World War, as well as during war's initial years.

The anti-Jewish "racial laws" — a by-product of fascist Italy's alliance with Germany known as the "Rome-Berlin Axis" — were promulgated in the summer of 1938. The racial laws targeted all Jews living in Italy at that time, both indigenous Italian Jews — mostly of Spanish or Italian origin dating back countless generations — and Jews living in territories acquired after Italy's victory in 1918 at the end of the First World War, for the most part border areas including Fiume, Trieste and Trento.

Despite these laws, and in keeping with its best human tradition, Italy gave refuge to Jews who escaped Germany after the Nazis came to power, as well as to those who had escaped Austria and Czechoslovakia after Hitler annexed Austria and forced Czechoslovakia to cede the

Sudetenland to Germany. Though in Italy on a transit base, most members of this latter category became part of the local Jewish communities, largely owing to the fact that the vast majority of countries in the world had closed their gates to Jewish immigration, even in the face of the oncoming catastrophe.

Under the new racial laws, if they had not been recognized citizens by 1919, Italian Jewish citizens lost their citizenship — an impossible situation for Jews like those living in Fiume, annexed to Italy only in 1924, after a short life as a "free city." Thus, when Italy joined the war on the side of Nazi Germany on June 10, 1940, hundreds of Jews living in places along the Italian borders (such as Fiume) were arrested, as well as thousands of foreign refugees, mostly Jews, who were now stateless. Italy's "solution" was to scatter all these "free interned" people among small villages, mainly in central and southern Italy — settlements off the beaten track in the mountains — where they could live as they liked, with was almost non-existent police control. Two or three families shared each home, and even received a kind of "monthly subsidy" paid by the government as a living allowance. Among the "free interned" were foreign enemy aliens, Italian political prisoners, and others condemned by the authorities.

Even during the war, Italy continued to save Jewish lives, such as the thousands of Jews escaping German and Croatian occupied territories. The Italians took them under their protection, transferring them inside their borders, some as "free interned" and some as prisoners in the

Ferramonti camp in Calabria, where they were ultimately liberated by the Allies in 1943.

This extraordinary situation came to an end on September 8, 1943, with the collapse of Italy. From that day on, the Germans took direct control of the areas not yet reached by the Allies, and set in motion their "Final Solution of the Jewish Problem."

During this period Jews from Fiume, including my family — my father, my mother, my brother and myself — were interned in a small village by the name of Navelli. At the time, I was 16 years old. I compiled this memoir immediately after we were liberated, hand-written in journal form in Italian, when the details were still very sharp in my mind. A few years later, I translated the manuscript into English, as a lasting legacy for my family in Kfar Warburg, and as a living testimony to the plight of Italian Jews during the *Shoah*.

The sketches that accompany this volume — drawn during the events described and the landscapes they document — are my own, for the most part penned on the back of postcards of the period, supplied to internees.

Luigi Fleischmann

September 1943

Navelli can be found easily on any good map of the Abruzzi region. It is a village of some 2,000 inhabitants, its contours not very different from many other mountain villages in the central Apennines. It hugs a slope crawling up to the crest of a hill where a typical medieval castle sits. The new part of the village, built with money sent home by native sons who emigrated to America, is situated partly in the Navelli plain and partly along the northern slope of the hill.

The village dominates a plain of perhaps six kilometers, extending to Collepietro from the entrance to Navelli and down to Civitaretenga at the rear — a geographical bottleneck about two kilometers to the north of Navelli. It is a narrow passage along which the road runs, dominated by Civitaretenga, part of the same local council as Navelli. Beyond this bottleneck lies another open plain that runs for another several kilometers, surrounded by hills just like the Navelli plain.

Navelli is situated more than 700 meters above sea level, northeast of the Gran Sasso mountain chain. To the south, the imposing massive peaks of the Majella Mountains dominate the horizon. Navelli itself sits on a crossroad linking the national highway from Aquila to

Popoli and Sulmona, and the provincial (seven-kilometer) road to Capestrano, Bussi and Pescara.

Our "colony" of interned people is a diverse group. We are three Jewish families — the Fleischmanns, the Degens and the Billigs. There is one British family — the Osmo-Morris's — two other British matrons, and a handful of political exiles such as Giordano Bruno from Tuscany, a former soldier in the Spanish civil war, and a Yugoslav by the name of Dusan.

Time lays heavy on our hands due to the monotony of doing nothing, but we remain quite healthy. We pass the morning hours visiting here and there. Daily at about 11 a.m., we must report at the local police station to be "counted" by the *Carabinieri*.[1] The officials come out, glance at us and, from time to time, even count our number. They then bark, "OK, you can go now!"

In the afternoon, we take a stroll up the surrounding hills, through ravines, the small woods and along the roads, although we have been forbidden to go beyond the last house of the village. But the *Carabinieri* turns a blind eye, saying that we are, after all, human beings, not wild animals to be kept in a cage. Time passes much in this fashion.

This has been my father's daily regime for years. It is now more than three years since that day — June 19, 1940, to be exact — when at 4 a.m. the Blackshirts[2] came

---

1   The gendarmerie and military police of Italy.
2   The Blackshirts (Italian: *camicie nere* or *squadristi*) were Fascist paramilitary groups in Italy during the period immediately fol-

with fixed bayonets to take him away from our home in Fiume. After detention in Fiume, Father was moved from one place to the next, together with more than 300 other local Jews. They were led away like criminals, but the fascist militiamen asked their forgiveness for such treatment, saying, "We are not guilty. We have to obey orders. Poor men." From Fiume they were sent to the camp in Nereto. From there they were taken to Notaresco near Teramo, and then to the hellish concentration camp in Ferramonti, Calabria. For the past 11 months — since October 1942 — he has been here in Navelli — classified as a "free interned" person. We — my mother, my little brother Livio and I — have been in Navelli since April, except for a short interlude in Fiume in June.

So here we live, in a farmer's house, in the lower part of Navelli, in the "newer section" of the town along the road to Capestrano. After Fiume, we find ourselves surrounded by mountains and simple farmers, among fields and sheep going to pasture — except for the daily "police parade."

The British internees — the Osmo-Morris family — live near the central square called S. Pelino. They are a very strange family. The head of the family is an excellent doctor. (Indeed, he treated Father very well last March for an attack of kidney colic.) He has a wife, two sons —

lowing World War I and until the end of World War II. The Black-shirts were organized by Benito Mussolini as a military tool of his Fascist movement. Their methods became harsher as Mussolini's power grew, and they used violence, intimidation, and murder against Mussolini's opponents.

15

Renato and George — a daughter — Dora — and an elderly mother. A strange family. Each accuses all the others of being mad, and all together they don't realize that they are all equally crazy. A very important "member of the family" is Lilla, their little dog. They have the misfortune of living in the house of a very zealous fascist, Don Ernesto Torlone. This is one of the reasons they are always arguing.

I am very friendly with George Osmo-Morris, and we all take very nice walks together. When talking and discussing things, he can be very amusing.

The Degen family lives in the middle of the village. They have two sons, Manfred and Enzo. In their house it is the wife, Recha, who is in charge, and who deals with the farmers. The husband — the good-hearted and serene but somewhat gossipy Sami — wanders around, engaging in some petty commerce, carrying water from the public fountain in the copper container, peeling potatoes and lighting the oven, thus making small profits that allow him to smoke some cigarettes. The other family — the Billigs — lives on the other side of Navelli, in the direction of Civitaretenga.

Due to the heat, we all sit in the square under the big chestnut trees, and I occupy myself listening to the arguments on communism between George, Bruno and Dusan.

For some months now we have been living in a state of near euphoria. The successful conclusion of the Tunisian campaign in North Africa, the Soviet victories on the Eastern front, the Allies' landings in Sicily, the downfall of Mussolini and the landings in Calabria all give us the feeling that liberation is not far away. After July 25 and the downfall of Mussolini, even the police have lost interest in continuing to "count" us. They take down the Savoia-fascist shield that adorned the entrance to the station, and in its place put the old pre-fascist shield back up — held in reserve for the last 21 years. Very provident people, these Italians!

We feel like we're literally walking on air, sure that the Italy of "the millions of bayonets" cannot prevail much longer. We can feel the change in the air — and not just in the metaphorical sense. On August 27, but a few days ago, we heard, for the first time, the heavy and powerful "wings of death" of Allied aircraft over our heads. A long convoy of American Flying Fortresses passed above us, generating fear in our hearts as our ears tingled with the vibration set off by the deep thunderous hum of their engines. This was the first manifestation of war and the approaching front. They were on their way to bomb Sulmona.

On September 8, 1943, Italy surrendered to the Allies. The news was met in our village — and I believe all over Italy for that matter — with the same disorder, dismay and bewilderment. But for us, this event could spell a swift liberation. Now, some days down the road, we have begun to examine other questions, conducting grandiose strategic arguments as to when the Allied armies will arrive and liberate us. We even put forward the idea of moving south toward Foggia or that vicinity, in the direction of the front. After all, the *Carabinieri* have abandoned the police station. But later we conclude that perhaps the Allies will be here before we will even have time to pack our bags.

George and Father believe that the German forces will withdraw to the north — to the valley of the Po River — and that the battle of Salerno still raging for the last three or four days is solely a holding action fought by the Germans to hold back the Allies and cover their own retreat.

I myself am less optimistic. Despite entreaties from all present not to break the aura of optimism, I hold that the Germans will not relinquish ground so suitable for a defensive line as central Italy so fast — a position from which they can wear down the Allies. And I add — half jokingly — that we shall only see the Allied forces in May. They all threaten to stone me.

20 SEPTEMBER 1943

For the past few days, the situation has become chaotic. We cannot fathom what is going on any more. The roads are full of former Italian soldiers, some going one way, some the other. Here in Navelli, there was a unit of some 25 soldiers attached to the air defense corps. They all left. I will always remember those particular soldiers because of something that happened back in the summer that gave us "food for thought" about the fighting spirit of our enemies. The soldiers were performing exercises on the small football field near our house. They were under the command of a lieutenant who looked a little like a priest — always holding a prayer book in his hands. The officer was giving his men orders to "hit the dirt," and the soldiers were pleading, "Sir, we can't! There are cactuses and stinging nettles." They simply balked at carrying out his orders. Mussolini's army. We were sitting near the road by Degen's neighbor Adolfo, a trader who, already in the wake of the Axis' defeat in Tunisia, took the insignia of the P.N.F (the National Fascist Party) off his shirt. Very clever.

The battle of Salerno has been won. The British are advancing from Foggia northward in the direction of S. Severo. We are optimistic. It cannot take very long for us to be liberated. Even some "politicals" leave. Dusan takes a loaf of bread, some cheese and a bottle of water and departs. He tells us, "I'll go up to Trieste, and then to Tito's partisans." Out of all the political internees, only Bruno remains. He has married the daughter of Pisciarola the baker and is working in the bakery, too. He sells the farmer's bread along with his Marxist and Leninist theories!

For two or three days now we have observed movement of military traffic on the national highway. Khaki-colored cars are speeding northward. We go there to have a look, secretly hoping to see insignias of Allied units, but later we observe that the cars have the sign "W.H."[3] on them. German units. From time to time, they stop to fill their water tanks and take souvenir photos, glancing sideways at the Italians, who gaze back at them with a combination of curiosity mixed with hate and contempt...and trepidation, too. They wear shorts and field caps with a broad peak. The

3   *Wehrmacht Heer*, from 1935 to 1945 the military section of the German Wehrmacht that also consisted of the navy and air force.

19

vehicles are covered with dust all the way to the roof, and all in all they look to me quite different — very different from those I saw passing through Fiume in 1941 on their way to occupy Yugoslavia.

I have gotten to know many new people, whom George introduced me to in the village. Having been interned here in Navelli for more than three years, he knows many people here. They all are very nice young men — all students who returned from the army after Italy's surrender. They were just young recruits, and their country has already collapsed in their faces. They all have very liberal outlooks, and are not at all fascist now.

We quickly become a group, and stroll together every evening. There is a chemistry student, Aurelio Alterio, small, with a big black mustache; Ugo Marrano, a literature major, a merry and well-liked fellow; Umbertino Cimetta, a tall, thin officer in the royal army; and Giuseppe Boccabella, whose father lives in Canada and who wanted to be sent to Tunisia as an anti-tank gunner so he could be taken prisoner and go to Canada too... Then there are two brothers, Piero and Iginio Quintilo. The latter is my age. Our discussions are long-winded and almost always about politics. Their heads are filled with far-reaching thoughts, but they fear for the future. They have no idea how to build an Italian democracy, and ignore almost everything that democracy means. George comments that they still reason too much with a fascist mindset, and they rightly reply that they were born in 1924–1925, under fascism. When they see Germans passing by, their faces cloud over. And the Germans pass more or less to the north.

In little villages rumors spread quickly, and from house to house they become more and more exaggerated. Today, a lone German on a motorcar stopped in the village with a flat tire. The farmers began to gather around him, and I could see that he was afraid of being alone. But he regained his confidence quickly when he realized that the Italians were helping him and not about to kill him. I took a walk with George up into the village, through the never-ending narrow lanes and stairs to reach the top where the post office is situated, to see if there was some mail for us — our daily climb for the mail. These are the important daily things: the coach and the mail. When we reached the top, farmers and women asked us what "the Germans" are doing down there, and others shouted that the Germans have already plundered the wheat store and were now climbing up into the village. They refused to believe us when we told them that there was only one German down there. There was no mail for us. When we returned to the lower part of the village, the farmers had already calmed down.

Every evening, together with the students, we go to the home of the Quintilo family to listen to the radio repeating, "Italians, this is the crucial week," and so on. We also hear that a fascist republic has been founded in the north, after the liberation of Mussolini, who was interned about 40 kilometers from here, on the Gran Sasso. This was perhaps ten days ago.

The Degens and the Billigs were very nervous when they saw all the Germans on the roads, but they felt somewhat reassured seeing them going northwards. It's easy to understand them. Mr. Billig has already been in

21

Dachau, but managed to get out thanks to some financial arrangement.

We celebrated the High Holidays at Degen's home. We didn't have ten people for a *Minyan*.[4] We were only five. We managed to pray, leaving out some parts of the service. It was Rosh Hashanah[5], and while praying we saw some German cars through the window stopping down in the lower part of the square. Billig and his son took off their prayer shawls and dashed out of the door, "explaining" that they were running to the upper reaches of the village in order to...have a better view. But those who remained did not feel very calm either.

We received the news — brought by Degen, back via the coach from a visit to the dentist — that the Germans have occupied Aquila with heavy forces and have begun to regulate and monitor people traveling on the postal coach. Aquila lies 37 kilometers away. We are now in the last days of September. It is not very hot any more in the countryside, and is actually quite cool in the evening. We are still very tense with the news on the radio. Now the British 8th Army is already nearing Campobasso. British commandos have landed at Termoli. In short, everybody says it will take perhaps two or three more weeks, but I don't believe it. I can see that the German defense is too stiff in the Marsica region — even if it is only German rearguard action, like the one that preceded the taking of

4 A traditional quorum of ten or more adult (over the age of 13) male Jews for the purpose of communal prayer.
5 Jewish New Year.

Napoli by Allied forces. Of course, the best thing would be a very swift liberation.

About noon, George came to visit us. (For many months, he always came after lunch.) What was the matter and what was the rush? Ah, nothing special. He had decided to go down south. Things were still chaotic to the south. In a couple of days, he could cover 100 kilometers, hide in some village where there is only a German rearguard, and then be freed when the Allies arrive. He showed us how he was all ready for the journey, and this made us laugh: two loafs of bread and jam and a bottle of water, all wrapped up in a woolen sweater full of holes "in order to be protected against the cold nights," although his girlfriend Adriana — a cheap girl from Genova — had decided to go with him. They gulped down half our lunch — two plates of *kartoffel knodel*[6] with sugar and poppy seeds.

Suddenly, we heard a noise coming from the road. Oh no! It was a Nazi motorized force. They were passing by on their way north. They were entering the village! At the head of the convoy was a patrol on motorcycles — exactly as I had seen for the last three years in newspaper photographs — dusty vehicles and men with grave faces. They advanced near our house, then turned back with their vehicles and entered the square, dismounted and started to ... shave and clean themselves up... We breathed a sigh of relief.

Later on, they affixed directional signs to the telephone poles along the main road, enquired about possible

6 Potato dumplings.

accommodation for troops, asked where the town hall was, and then took off in the direction of Capestrano. They combed every village and hamlet in the vicinity in the same fashion. We now find ourselves in the middle of German-occupied territory, no longer the "no-man's-land" that was Italy for the last three weeks. We face printed proclamations on the walls signed "OKW Kesserling,"[7] threatening death to anyone bearing arms or trying to oppose German forces "restoring order".

I can see that the farmers are somewhat scared, but on the whole they want nothing to do with the fascists. They still don't know how to behave with these new rulers. They don't know them yet. They have already finished threshing the wheat and are now starting to harvest the grapes, and really nothing else interests them.

My brother went with our landlord and the donkey to harvest the grapes in a little vineyard on a hillside. They returned home with very good grapes. George, agonizing for some days about his alternatives — "Today I leave" — "Tomorrow I leave" — finally decided not to leave, but to

---

7 *Oberkommando Wehrmacht Kesserling.* Albert Kesserling served as general field marshal of the air force and later commander-in-chief of the German troops in Italy during World War II. His noteworthy military and strategist career was marred by his involvement in the Ardeantine cave massacre of March 1944, in which 335 Italian civilians were shot. Kesserling finished the war on the western front. A British military court in Venice sentenced Kesserling to death in 1947 for killing Italian hostages, but his sentence was commuted to life imprisonment. He was released due to ill health in October 1952 and died on July 16, 1960, in Bad Nauheim.

24

change his place of residence. From the lower part of the village, he went into hiding in the very old part of Navelli, on the slopes of the mountain — amidst a labyrinth of little streets perhaps no more than 50 centimeters wide, stinking and muddy. He found a cellar-like place with two rooms. He told me that it was "not because I fear the Germans, but because I do not want to see them"...

The farmers protested (against whom exactly?) because some Nazi soldiers stole some ripe grapes along the main road. We celebrated our Yom Kippur fast, extremely worried about what the future holds for us.

We now have a new *Carabinieri* commanding officer — but without *Carabinieris*. The new *Carabinieri* is lame, walks with the help of a stick and goes around without his uniform. On his right arm, he wears an armband — a white background with the word *Polizei* emblazoned across it. But we can see that at least so far, he doesn't want to even know about the presence of interned Jews or British. The previous police officer picked up and left without soldiers or orders to do so — "dismissing himself." He was a fat man. (All the Italian police officers I've encountered are fat.) This one was Sicilian, but very cowardly. He left with his wife and two children, not wishing to have anything to do with the Germans.

October 1943

In the last few months, my father has become acquainted

with advocate Piero Santucci — nephew of a General Santucci from Navelli. (This general, despite the Allies already being in Sicily, told the farmers: "We of the Axis already have victory in our pockets!") Santucci is a landowner here.

Santucci introduced my father to a Neapolitan antique dealer who was evacuated here with his family in the wake of the bombing — the very honorable Tullio Giosi, a cheerful guy, typically Neapolitan. Father teaches him German, for a fee of course, because the daily subsidy for interned people — eight lire — is no longer arriving. This is in addition to a kind of "school" he has been running every morning for the past year, teaching Italian to Degen's two sons and the son of Billig — Manfred — with school books brought from Fiume by my brother Livio. He does all this because he hates to see those boys growing up like savages. But in this case, he does it for free, of course.

We don't get any more newspapers. Without the radio, every evening we would be lost, indeed.

We are already in the first week of October, and it's quite cool. We still await the Allies. This morning, we were awakened by a new kind of "show," a really interesting one at that: an air raid by Allied fighter-bombers. The noise of airplanes and explosions woke us up. We ran to the windows just in time to see a British fighter hurtling over our heads at breakneck speed, almost brushing the tops of the roofs, then climbing for altitude. Four other planes on the tail of the lead plane followed him up into the skies like a chain. There was a thundering screech, and four machine guns opened up, accompanied by the sound of piercing whistles and explosions. Perhaps four or five fighters were attacking a convoy of German trucks. Farmers ran out of their houses in fright, but the attack had a comic side as well: in front of us lives a cross-eyed woman, Minchelina, who is always cursing and hitting her husband who is twice her age. She ran out very frightened, yelling, "Oh Madonna Mia! If they could only kill you!" Then, seeing a fighter plane diving down with a shriek strafing targets and almost shaving the tops of the trees, *she* shrieked and ran back into her house! After some more of this "merry-go-round" the planes departed.

There are always many discussions during my daily walks with George and the students. Aurelio has shown himself to be the most truly anti-fascist. He is actually a communist ideologically. Our arguments focus on politics, and what interests us most of all is the military situation at the frontline.

It seems that the Allies are taking their time. A week after the occupation of Napoli, they are barely at Caserta and Capua; and here, on the Adriatic side of the mountains, they advance even slower. Campobasso and Vasto-Istonio are in their hands, but it looks like the German defense is stiffening more and more. All of these meetings and discussions look to me more and more like conspiracies than anything else. And indeed, they reveal to me — although I am too young and it's questionable whether I would be able to commit myself — that they have decided to form a group of "patriots," the same way that groups like this are being formed all over Italy. According to Radio Tunis (an Allied army station) some of these groups in Lazio and Toscana have even become guerrilla units.

They've discovered where those 25 Italian soldiers buried their weapons before scattering to all four winds: in a courtyard along the main road, where a German road maintenance unit generally stays overnight. They say that in order to do something real, we need to obtain weapons. I agree with them. We have to secretly find those arms before somebody reveals them to the Germans, if we are to avoid those promised executions.

9 OCTOBER 1943

Yesterday evening, the "group" went in to action. George Osmo-Morris was there, along with Bruno, the students and some farmers with the same ideas — such as Luigi Alterio and Torlone. Accompanied by donkeys with big baskets on their backs and digging tools, we started to dig in the courtyard. While it was surrounded by high walls, we were at risk of being discovered by the German road patrol. George feared that the youngsters were taking this "caper" too lightheartedly. They still didn't know who the Germans were and what they were capable of doing. Only two months ago they were war allies with them!

After one hour's work, we had dug out three light machine-guns, eight Mitra-type sub-machine guns and

16 rifles. With no time to sort them out, we loaded the weapons and the crates onto the patiently waiting donkeys. We exited the village with difficulty, leading the donkeys through the dark for about two kilometers. We descended into a very deep ravine called "paradise of the donkeys" by the local farmers, because that's where they throw the carcasses of dead donkeys. We stashed the weapons and crates in a cave along a crack of the ravine, and covered them up with canvasses to keep them dry from the water dripping all over the place. The three machine guns each come with a box of tools and implements, a reserve barrel and 6,000 rounds of ammunition. The crates contain 4,000 rounds for the Mitra sub-machine guns and several thousand bullets for the rifles. There are 60 hand grenades as well, but only one magazine for the sub-machine guns. We discarded a heavy Fiat machine gun because there was no ammunition for it. At about 9 p.m. we returned to the village and went to listen to the radio.

The "colony" of interned people has lived here without any big worries — until now. The Germans pass up and down the road, but so far nobody has taken any notice of our being here. We continue to wait it out.

10 OCTOBER 1943

This morning we were in for a bad surprise. The road was blocked by a very long line of cars and trucks. The square, too. Germans were everywhere. What was happening?

A German unit was occupying the village and settling in wherever they could.

We observed the whole thing together with Mr. Degen, who had come to tell Father when he could slaughter a sheep at Settimio's place. We observed, somewhat nervously, the Germans setting about getting situated. They were all very busy parking trucks and cars and unloading crates. We went out to find out who and what they were. The signs they put up at the entrance of the village said: "BACKERKOMPANIE FPN 1 21063." So, they are bakers attached to the Luftwaffe, the bakers of the whole 1st Paratrooper's Division. I saw officers running up and down. The farmers began to mumble, because they noticed the Germans occupying stables. The soldiers pushed out two nicely fat pigs without asking anybody, slaughtered the animals and roasted them by hanging them with a rope from a tree. The farmers grumbled even more — this time with fear when they realized that with all this concentration of trucks, ovens on wheels and soldiers at a quick glance one could conclude that there must be around 200 men here. The village could become an inviting target for Allied fighter-bombers.

The Nazis have been here in the village for some days now, but it seems the immediate danger has passed. They don't seem to care about us. Anyway, to be sure and to calm ourselves, in the morning, together with Aurelio and Ugo, I went to the abandoned former *Carabinieri* police station to see if there were any documents left — papers concerning Jews and British nationals. Nothing was left. We also went down to the cellar to see if perhaps we could find some magazines for the four Mitras, but we came up empty handed.

I don't believe that these youngsters have any actual plans to start any guerrilla actions that would be of any importance. The British are advancing slowly. They have been held up for a couple of days and seem unable to cross a small watercourse running parallel to the Sangro River. For the moment, all the kids want is for the weapons to be in the hands of people who in due time will use them well.

Father told us that he was able to teach only half a lesson of German to Mr. Giosi at Santucci's home because the Germans had taken over the house — almost all the best rooms — as a billet for the *kommandatur* with two captains, one lieutenant, and clerks with a radio, oven and office equipment. The two men promised Father that they will keep secret from the Nazis the presence of three families in Navelli who know how to speak German and Italian and, on top of it all, are Jewish.

One evening, as we were sitting in the Osmo-Morris home, we heard that escaped English POWs had appeared at the outskirts of the village. We ran quickly to intercept them before they ended up in the midst of the Germans. I went with George, and of course Adriana joined us. There were three British and one huge Australian with blue eyes. George took them to his house where they washed up. Later, they had an evening meal at the home of Miss Moldenhower, the interned English woman. The next morning, before they left for the south, I brought the escapees a nice road map of Italy "courtesy of the Touring Club," hoping it would help them somehow.

Now I generally pass my day sitting in the square, by the door of the "house of the English," together with Miss Osmo-Morris and their daughter Dora and son Renato, a medical student, and with Ugo or Giuseppino. At the same time, we observe the Germans and their movements. We have noted that among the Germans are men with worn-out uniforms without any insignias, and non-German looking faces. One of our group — Nicola who is sitting with us — had served in Russia as a soldier, and recognized by their speech that they were Russian. With his few broken words in Russian, we asked them something. They were POWs, made to work by the Germans. But I saw that these must be very mild-mannered Germans, since the Russians were not doing very much and were quite merry.

In the evening, during my usual walk with my friends through the square and the lower part of the village, we heard very sad accordion music together with singing coming from a long, low building — a sort of sports gymnasium, not far from our house. It sounded like a lamentation. We summoned our courage and went in. The sentry didn't say anything. Inside there were about 20 Russians, some of them sprawled on the floor, singing. A Ukrainian was playing the accordion and singing in Russian — his eyes closed and a smile on his face. In front of him, a Cossack and a Mongolian-looking guy were dancing in quick steps and leaps, accompanied by rhythmical handclapping by the rest of the Russians. As we stood gazing at the gathering, an elderly captain entered the building and shouted at us in German, "*Rauss*!" We left.

14 October 1943

The morning began for us in a very anxious way. My
mother and I had just returned from the water fountain.
(We always go in pairs because Mother cannot carry the
water container on her head like the native women.) A
German soldier suddenly entered the kitchen, saluted and
told us — "The interned person Fleischmann must present
himself at 13:30 at the German command!" "The interned
person Fleischmann?!" Mother was very worried. When
my father returned from the Degens' house and heard the
news, he told me to come with him. We went back to the
Degens'. There we found George Osmo-Morris' father,
worried, too. Father told them what had happened; he was
unable to decide whether to go or not. The other two were
also deep in thought. If he did not present himself, the
Nazis might start a search. If he went, who knows what
could happen?! Father decided to go after all, and take me
with him. Doing so, he would give the others the possibility
of remaining unseen and, hopefully, even provide a way
to alert them if things should go badly. The "war council"
adjourned and everyone headed home. We were nagged
by the question — how do they know about "the internee
Fleischmann?"

14 October 1943: 1.30 p.m.

We had a very nerve-wracking lunch. After a two-minute

33

walk, we reached the Santuccis' house and entered the German command post. We could hear orders being shouted in a hoarse voice, the noise of typewriters, soldiers and warrant officers coming and going. At least the door of the command office was open, and we were invited to come in. Father and I were naturally very tense and agitated. It was a very large room, perhaps six meters long and more than three meters wide, furnished with carpets and paintings. A big fireplace warmed the room, even though we were only in the middle of October. On a small table to the right sat a radio, and we could hear very soft military music coming out of the speaker. In the center there was an oval table. A German captain met us. He was dressed in his blue air-force uniform, closed all the way up to his neck, and was wearing spectacles. He looked about 60, a little chubby and of medium height. He greeted my father in German. A tall, young captain and a young lieutenant with a very Nazi face stood up, as well. The captain introduced himself as *Hauptmann* Ehrig from Magdeburg, a professor; the other one as captain Corn from Nuremberg; and the third one as lieutenant *Oberzahlmeister* Peters, from Berlin. Captain Ehrig invited us to sit down. His personal driver and batman[8] — a fellow called Bergen — was also sitting in the room, looking at us. Father and I were quite scared to find ourselves facing these three German officers with a swastika on their breasts.

Captain Ehrig started by saying that he knows my father's "situation." I doubt if the other two know anything,

8 A soldier assistant assigned to an officer.

because they were not paying any attention to what was going on; Corn even got up and left. Captain Ehrig said he would do nothing that may harm my father. But since he had heard (through whom?) that we knew some German, he had taken the liberty of asking us to help him a little in his daily dealings with the Italians (what an honor!). In short, he was asking us to be some sort of translators, and added again that "he would strive to act in a way that would not compel my father to behave contrary to his beliefs," concluding, "I understand all very well." Father pushed me forward, saying that I was quite young and could do much more work (but did not say that my knowledge of German was quite poor). Captain Ehrig agreed and told me to come every afternoon if I liked, between 3-5 p.m., in order to translate what he wanted to say. In the meantime, he turned me over to *Feldwebel* (warrant officer) Heinz, tall and with a small, blond mustache, who jumped to attention, clicking his heels with a sharp metallic clack. *Jawohl*! On the spot, I had to translate something to the lame shoemaker and saddle-maker Mario — about how he must mend some truck covers.

In the evening at the "war council," my now "former intern" father reported to everyone what had happened. Degen, as well as the English people, and particularly George, were receptive to the idea and were even somewhat glad to have almost a bridgehead to information about the movements of the opponent.

I told the story later to the "gang" in George's cellar-house. Here, too, the response was the same.

There is a lot to be translated in a German command post,

some of it quite interesting. It is raining and the weather is cool. Present at the post today were the *Carabinieri* officer, in uniform (what happened to his brain?); Doctor Falconio, the local secretary of the fascist party (the old party one, not the new "republican" one); De Guido, the secretary of the local council; and old General Santucci, whom I suspected was the source of this nice "joke" of summoning us to the Germans. Captain Ehrig made me translate his wishes: he intended to cooperate and wanted the others to cooperate, as well, meaning to graciously obey his wishes: to maintain the curfew from 8 p.m., to occupy Baron Francesconi's manor house, to house a battery of ovens there, and to turn over a third of the wheat stored in the village's grain collection point from the last harvest. A group of 30 men should be on reserve to serve as workers in case of an "enemy" air attack. He will pay these workers if and when they are needed and promised to behave in a suitable manner towards the people of the village of Navelli.

The Italians looked at each other, amazed at this lovely form of "cooperation," whereby one side gives the orders and the other side has to carry them out. They muttered a few curses in Italian, but asked me not to translate — something I would not have done in any case. The Captain shook the hand of each participant, snapping his heels and bowing his head. They just bowed their heads in response, and left. What else could they do?

This morning *Feldwebel* Heinz asked permission from my father to let me go with him by car to Aquila to help him translate. We left in an army Volkswagen. Within 40 minutes, I was in Aquila.

It was the first time I had seen the place. I immediately liked the town, with its *corso*[9] and covered walks, the wide marketplace and the *villa*[10] — the modern and well-shaded part of this town. I went around with the German to various army posts. Then he asked me to go with him to a big store to buy nails. In the evening, we returned to Navelli. It is quite risky to travel by day with a car. You have to do so quickly because of the fighter-bombers.

Every day now we meet in the morning with the whole group at George's "home" in the heart of the old village, amidst the small lanes, narrow passages, arches and stairs. We argue and comment mainly about the military situation. They ask me what is happening at the Nazi command post, and I happily give them a detailed report.

They have no intention yet of taking any action whatsoever. It would be irrational and of no use, really. It is only this morning that we read, pasted on the walls of the village, a poster signed *Kesserling - Oberbefehlshaber Sud* which announced that six "bandit" Italians, all officers of the "Royal army," were caught with arms in their hands, captured and executed in Popoli.

In the evening at Quintilo's home, we listened to the radio — the "Voice of London," the "Voice of Tunis," the "Voice of America." The Americans have at last reached the Garigliano River in some places, and the British face Castel di Sangro and the estuary of the river Sangro, near Pescara. Not all that much closer, but only 60

9   Paths
10 Hall

kilometers as the crow flies. Perhaps with one or two more offensives...

Traffic and movement on the main road fluctuates. Some days it's quite heavy, some days less. Supplies are moved up to the battle line by day and night. By day, the road is policed by armored vehicles with anti-aircraft guns. The farmers are filled with wonderment and admiration at the sight of these tracked vehicles and the weaponry. In spite of this, in the last days of October, we again experienced two very heavy air strafings. The fighters, though they only discovered one car, attacked it. Below Collepietro, a lone car was strafed, and an officer was killed in an incident beyond Civitaretenga, as well. Groups of fighters roar over Navelli almost every day — all of them Allied planes.

To date, they have not discovered the traffic in the village proper, nor the smoke from the bakeries in Francesconi's backyard, where ovens produce 10,000 loaves of bread a day — square loaves of black bread. It's a pity they have not spotted them. *That* would have been a pretty show — and a constructive contribution to the war effort!

Our lives go on with the same monotonous routine, the only change being the "local" Germans and my "job." Livio continues to prepare the wood and light the cooking fire at home; Mother cooks, prepares the bread and takes it to the bakery; and Father goes on with his German lessons with Santucci and Giosi, and goes to Degen's.

A few days ago, Father went to Captain Ehrig with a request that the German command pay the farmers for the two pigs taken on the day the unit arrived. Although when taking the pigs away the soldiers said to the farmers, "Badoglio will pay,"[11] Captain Ehrig agreed. He paid 1,400 lire for each pig. Not bad.

In any case, the farmers are much calmer, now. The Captain gave an order for a big warning sign to be put at the entrance of the village, in German, prohibiting any German soldier from entering any home during the night without a written permit from the local command and forbidding stealing or commandeering anything from civilians without a direct order.

We still met on Saturday, as before, at the Degen's house to pray. Anyway, Germans rarely appear in those narrow lanes with all those stairs.

We are now at the end of October. The weather is a little better now. Today Heinz and another warrant officer, Spiess — who looks and talks like a fanatical Nazi and wears not only the shield of the SA but also the insignia of the Nazi party (N.S.D.A.P) on the breast of his uniform — took me on a ride with a command car to the south. I had the chance to see a host of interesting things. We passed Popoli, and then drove in the direction of Sulmona. After an hour, we were more than 40 kilometers away from Navelli—traveling southeast. The two Germans conversed continually about the same thing: "Look at those Italians, those *Scheissers*. *Scheissers* are dirtier than the Russians. Traitors. People of sheep." Ranting on like that. Every five to ten minutes, they stopped the car and listened for airplanes. By chance, not even one flew over today. I was

11 Pietro Badoglio, premier of Italy (1943–1944).

not so disappointed, because I could have been caught "in the middle of it" as well. I'm not such a hero to want to die together with two Germans. Heinz, nevertheless, seems to be a fairly decent guy, and I believe that he, like Captain Ehrig, knows about the "internee Fleischmann." Not the other German. Only that Heinz, when he calls me, always says, "Herr Schneider...ach excuse me, Herr Fleischmann!" He never remembers my name.

After a few more kilometers, beyond Pràtola Peligna, I started to understand the sector we were crossing. There were almost no Italians left. An uncanny quiet hung in the air. To the left and right of the road were many cars camouflaged with green netting, and some soldiers.

We took a side road, and under some bushes some German soldiers, still wearing shorts although it is mid-October, were working around a fuel dump. Heinz and Spiess went into a shack, filled up, and off we went again. The area was eerily silent. It was immediately to the rear of the front line, but one couldn't hear a thing. I believe that even they were tired of firing guns! We returned in the evening via the Bussi road. I cannot understand why they took me on this tour. There was really nothing to translate.

In the evening we listened to the radio again, and after the news, music. The broadcasts of the "Republican radio" don't interest us.

One afternoon, while descending by car with *Feldwebel* Heinz along the serpentines of the road at Barisciano (900 m.) leading to the valley of S. Gregorio in the direction of Aquila, Heinz stopped in order to admire the beautiful scenery — the valleys surrounded by mountains that stretch on and on, bathed in the light of the sunset. When we continued our descent again, he asked me whether there was another plain on the other side of the Gran Sasso. I answered, "No, the chain of the Apennines extends for another 300 kilometers at least, until you reach the plain." He sighed with disappointment. "What a pity," he said, and drove on.

The supply pipeline for the battle line passes through Navelli. At the crossroads, part of the traffic goes south in the direction of Castel di Sangro, the rest turns east to the front near Pescara, under Ortona.

My shoes are terribly worn out and have been resoled three times. They are low-cut shoes, city shoes that I had worn already in Fiume. How shall I manage now, with the rainy season upon us? And with the oncoming winter fast approaching? Winter is quite tough here…and as my father says, Who knows what else awaits us? I envy George, who has such a fine brand new pair of British army boots in his wardrobe!

NOVEMBER 1943

If we did not listen to the radio, I believe our morale would be very low. Especially Father. He sees the winter approaching, and the situation not getting better. The Germans seem very restrained right now, but one day they could seriously turn against us. As for the Allies, now he doubts there will be a quick liberation. Our means for sustaining ourselves are dwindling, and who knows for how long we will be able to continue.

We received a letter from Fiume written by one of our neighbors, Mrs. Zeisler. It was dated October 18. She told us they are very worried, but so far, nothing has happened. They have housed the Tutti family in our apartment so the Nazis or the republican fascists won't take over the empty place.

Each afternoon, at about 2 or 3 p.m., I go to the office of the command post. I do the usual things. A recent order forbids any of the residents of Navelli from leaving the village without a permit from the German command post. They are very busy, of course. During the whole afternoon, scores of farmers arrive to ask for these permits, and Captain Ehrig collects one lira per permit. A German clerk writes the permits, a very unpleasant sort of bloke with glasses and a shaven skull; he looks alot like Himmler. Captain Ehrig wants me to teach him some words in Italian so that he will be able to manage alone in case I would not want to come any more. He doesn't succeed in remembering even a single word.

It is raining and raining. All the days are gray — typical of November. Such rain in a village is no picnic: everything gets muddy, and in Navelli, with its countless flights of steps, the rain creates little "Niagara Falls" that carry with them all the dung, straw and garbage, with the water running down from the upper levels of Navelli into the square and the low lying sections at the base of the village.

In the house opposite ours, Michelina conducts business dealings with the German soldiers. She has a daughter, and the soldiers like to come to her. They bring bread — a good commodity to barter with. However, the farmers are not fond of bread made of bran and rye.

6 NOVEMBER 1943

This evening, after listening to the radio as usual, I brought home with me news of a big victory: the Red Army has liberated Kiev and is advancing along the entire front. Father sighed and said, "What a pity we're not in Kiev!" But we are here. Every evening, we all meet around the radio, every morning, at George's place. One morning, they dismantled an Italian hand grenade, a red-colored "Breda." They emptied it, and then reassembled it again, and that's how — inside the four walls of a room — we sort of learned how to use it.

Last Saturday, something very scary happened to us. We were praying *Mussaf* [12] in Degen's house. As usual, we had all gathered together and placed our prayer shawls around our shoulders. Someone knocked at the door, and before we could dispose of everything, General Santucci entered...and behind him *Feldwebel* Heinz! Everybody in the room turned pale — especially Billig, who almost fell

12 Additional prayer service (from the Hebrew word "to add"), said on the Jewish Sabbath and major holidays.

across a chair, he was so panic stricken. Heinz looked at us, saw the Hebrew prayer books and the prayer shawls, but didn't say a word. He saw other people who could speak German too, but remained quiet. General Santucci wanted me to go at once with Heinz to help him deal with some Italian workers who were putting down a water pipeline to the German bakery. I left. This cursed General Santucci! Could he not have waited until we had all left? And had it not been for Heinz, had it been another German with him, we could have been finished for good! But we remained very worried for the rest of the day, until we saw that nothing had happened…meaning Heinz had not talked. Thank goodness he was a pure Prussian!

Father still gives his lessons. Giosi helps us find cheap food. He's always happy and always on the lookout for food. When he walks about he is always singing, "*Vivere, Vivere,*" (To live, to live) and it seems that the Germans do not bother him. He always says, "What dumbos they are!" then goes back to singing and looking for food. He has two nice children.

We have a painter here in Navelli — the very honorable Mr. Cannata from Calabria. He paints well but is a very unpleasant person. When he visits, Captain Ehrig is exasperated and disgusted by Cannata's slick manner and bootlicking tactics to a point where the cold and dignified German is ready to give him a swift kick (thus, Ehrig tells his batman). Mr. Cannata is a personal enemy of Giosi, who is an antiquarian, while he, Cannata, is a painter.

It is raining and the roads are full of mud. Father and Livio were walking along a muddy road towards

Settimio's house to slaughter a sheep, forced to trudge through the mud to get there. Captain Corn passed by in a commandeered Fiat 1500, saw Father and Livio, stopped, and asked, "Mr. Fleischmann, do you want a lift in the car?" Father evaded the invitation, telling him he was almost there.

I almost like sitting at the German command post now because it is nicely heated. There is unending movement the whole afternoon — orders, soldiers, farmers.

Today we had a meeting with the local council. General Santucci was there, De Guido the secretary and the flat-footed mayor of the village. Many different things were discussed. The Captain asked how much grain was still in the central storehouse. The three Italians asked me to translate that they really didn't know. They had to check first. Then the General asked for funds to run the postal service, and then blurted out — explaining in French — that "one has to take in account the subsidy money for the interned people, too!"

What a jerk! What an idiot! The secretary and the town mayor looked at me with anxious eyes. Captain Ehrig's fingers were drumming on the table, but Lieutenant Peters — in a very faint voice — asked me to explain, "Who are these interned people?" General Santucci realized his blunder but was at a loss how to answer. In a brilliant stroke, I butted in and explained to Lieutenant Peters that the General meant the families of the Italians interned in England who had to get their government subsidies. Everybody was relieved.

Lieutenant Peters is quite a strange sort of man. My

father told me not to trust him — he looks like a Nazi. When he saw him, Father made quite a detour, keeping his distance as much as possible. Peters has an elongated face, blond hair and is always wearing his field cap with the broad peak, a leather jacket with an Iron Cross and his rank, trousers and boots like a riding instructor, and he carries a small whip in one hand. He is thin but not very tall, and when he talks he always has a very scornful and mocking air to him. From his conversations with Captain Ehrig, I gather he is a committed Nazi. God forbid!

At Quintilo's house, after the news on the radio from London or "Radio Bari," we listened to music. But the students do not let me "handle" the radio anymore because I prefer military marches, while they want jazz or soft music which I don't like.

The news, from our standpoint of course, is now somewhat better: the 8th Army has now started an attack south of the Sangro River and, at some points, has succeeded in advancing on the Sulmona sector to the southern slopes of the Majella, almost under our nose. But between us lays the Majella, and that is one remarkable mountain!

At George's home, every morning and evening, before going to listen to the news on the radio, we have a lot of discussions about how we can help the war effort, e.g., how we can puncture car tires with nails or pieces of glass. We have the instruction booklet on how to use the "Mitra" sub-machine gun as well. I am personally not very interested in this weapon. Aurelio is breaking his head trying to think where he can possibly get his hands on some dynamite or mines. We talk about the "beauty" and the necessity of finding some contact with a British agent or some partisan group that has started to be active in the Majella Mountains. But where can we find them?

On the main road, there is the usual traffic. But despite all the icy wind of November, the Germans now position someone to sit up against the windshields of the cars as they move forward, perched on the front of each vehicle, to detect the noise of any approaching British airplanes — something they couldn't do sitting inside the closed cars.

I have been to Aquila again, this time with a different *Feldwebel*, the one in charge of the bakeries. We went to bring flour from a mill. I saw how those poor Russians have to work for two hours carrying no less than a 100-kilo bag on each shoulder.

At first, I feared they would suspect me, seeing me with the Germans. But from their eyes I could tell that they did not consider me an enemy, and perhaps even understood my situation. They always maintain good relations with the villagers, and I believe that Navelli's people are quite open in talking to them — not like the contacts they have with the Germans. Captain Ehrig even let the farmers know that he does not like their contacts with the Russians. They are, after all, POWs. But the Italians don't pay much heed to this, and they are right!

In the afternoon the mail coach arrived — all riddled with bullet holes, and its passengers terrified. British fighters strafed it when the bus got mixed up in a German convoy. This caused one fatality and two severely wounded among the Italian passengers. Three other Nazi trucks were set on fire by the fighter planes. Among the passengers on the coach was Ugo Marrano's girlfriend. She was safe, but thoroughly shook up. We decided not to meet anymore on Saturday for prayers at the Degens' house. The Billigs are very afraid to come; something much more serious than last time could happen to us.

Today Captain Ehrig wanted me give him a tour of Navelli. He took Peters and Heinz with him. We all climbed the endless steps, and I took them through the worst lanes and streets with the hope that they would have enough after only one look. The one who cursed and panted more than anybody else was Heinz. He was ranting, having to constantly cross little creeks and stumble over broken stairs. We reached the top of the castle where there is a beautiful view. From the south, the Majella looks a lot closer the more you climb. From where we stood, we could hear thumps and rumbles, some isolated and some in unison: very clearly gunfire. It's the front line. We can already hear it — here in Navelli.

That made me very happy. But Heinz the Prussian exploded, "*Sacrament noch ein mahl!*" (Darn it, once again!). Hearing this, Lieutenant Peters turned and laughed. Then we went back down.

In the evening, as usual, we listened to the radio.

What are the British, namely the Osmo-Morris family doing? Well, nothing special, as usual. They still live in the house of Don Ernesto Torlone and bicker with him. Almost every day, while passing by, I look in and have a chat with them.

I was passing through upper Navelli when I saw

Lieutenant Peters and Captain Corn resting on the low wall. Cannata the painter was there, too. He wanted to confer his compliments to the two German officers, but was unable to speak their language and, seeing me on my way to George's house, called me over to translate that he wanted to give a painting to Captain Ehrig as a gesture. The Lieutenant asked, *"Und wass will noch dieser schesser?"* (And what else does this bastard want?)! I took my leave of all three.

At George's place, there was a "guest." I wondered how he found his way there. He was a German sergeant, a paratrooper, and was trying to make himself understood by George and Aurelio. When he saw me he was very glad to have somebody who could understand him. I believed that he was slightly drunk; he talked on and on. He declared that the war was lost, and the Russians were advancing. I made myself dumb and replied, "How come? I haven't heard anything." He answered, revealing the exact positions on the eastern front. Then he went on sobbing, and told us that in an air raid on Köln his children and wife were killed. "I am now alone in the world. Do you understand? And I don't know what to do anymore — why should I go on living?" We thought to ourselves, "Who asked you to?" but George and Aurelio grunted something in reply. Despite that, he really made one pity him. He added, "The war will be over by May. If not, I'll hang myself!" Then he staggered out, mumbling to himself, *"Ich hänge mich auf, in May, ich hänge mich auf!"* (I'll hang myself, in May, I'll hang myself!)

Because of the bad weather, the Germans of the unit

have been digging trenches to put the trucks inside, planning to cover them with some kind of roofing to hide them from Allied aircraft. In doing so, they have turned the main square into a big garage with moats.

In one of the German lessons, Giosi and Santucci told Father that Lieutenant Peters — who speaks French with them — had a very long conversation with them, speaking against the Jews and assuring Giosi and Santucci that, "if by chance he finds some, he would kill them with his own hands. They are pigs, miserable dogs, those Jews!" The Italians related all this to us, very worried for Father…who, of course, shared their worries. He was right in doubting Peters' cordiality. But it seems that despite everything, he remains ignorant of our true identity.

It has been raining again, and my shoes have rotted away completely. Today, in order to go to Aquila with a German officer and Berber the batman, I had to wear a pair of slippers and over them rubber galoshes. It was very uncomfortable in the army vehicle. Water entered from all sides, but at least there was no danger of air attacks. The weather was too bad. In Aquila, the car stopped before some army store and Berber remained with me. He talked. He said that he was from Berlin, a piano player. Then he asked me, "how come I talk German," giving me a suspicious look. I told him some cock-and-bull story that in Fiume one learns three languages, Italian, German and Slav, the inheritance of the Austria-Hungarian empire, and that more or less everybody speaks some German. He didn't seem convinced and asked me persistently whether I had ever been to Vienna. What was he driving at? I had, but of course I didn't tell him that for clearly "racial" reasons — that he shouldn't suspect I was Jewish. He persisted, but I answered in the negative. Then, believing me less and less, he gave up asking questions.

Again, the news from the radio is not encouraging. Things seem quite hopeless now. The British 8th Army has stopped at the Sangro River and at the foot of the Majella, facing the Nazi "winter line." It looks as if they have stopped for the winter. But we hope against hope that it will not be for long.

I am not at home most of the day, only for lunch and at night. In the morning, I frequent George's place or stroll around with the gang in the upper part of the village, where one rarely sees German soldiers. They always congregate around their bakery. We discuss everything, but mainly the thing that interests us most: what we should do to assist the war effort. There is the communist, Bruno, who wants to finish up the whole business. He claims with disgust that "one can't work with these students;" that in his opinion, first of all we have to prepare all the farmers, ideologically and spiritually, for passive resistance against the Nazis. The group, headed by George Osmo-Morris, prefers a small group — based in the village — that would be active in sabotage operations and would hit only by night and against objectives large and far enough away from the village in order to eliminate the risk of cruel retaliations against fellow inhabitants of Navelli (the Germans take revenge on ten Italians for every German killed). I, too, believe this to be the best path — at least as long as the fighting line is relatively distant from us

51

(about 50 kilometers), and static. Meanwhile, we pass the time playing cards or *Morra*, around the warm fireside in George's house.

In one of the last meetings with the representatives of the village, Captain Ehrig requested some food supplies, *"Und die Herren werden so gut sein und kollaborieren nicht wahr?"* (And the gentlemen will be as kind as to collaborate, isn't that so?) Naturally, the leaders of the community tried not to "collaborate." Ehrig wanted to do it in a very peculiar way: he demanded every farmer bring a cup of olive oil, one onion and 4 or 5 potatoes — every week. The idea is nothing to sneeze at. After all, there are 2,000 people living here in Navelli, and the Captain has thought up a brilliant way to get all he needs: who would mind giving one, only one, cup of oil or one onion a week? This is so funny that everybody could, indeed, bring more. And actually, the farmers bring what is requested — some bringing more than even two cups of oil, laughing at these stupid Germans who want only "one cup of oil and one onion!"...

The "gang" and George tried to break into the wheat storehouse in order to take away as much as they can, in lieu of the Germans taking it, with plans to distribute it among the population. But they were unable to open the gate, and shooting the lock could have alarmed the sentries. So they had to withdraw.

Navelli now has its first water pipeline, thanks to the Germans. But they use it, quite naturally, for their own benefit. They carry it from the spring, bringing running water into all the buildings they use, but more importantly, to the batteries of their baking ovens. These ovens work around the clock.

In the Francesconi's courtyard, a line of Nazi soldiers was practicing saluting a make-believe "officer." The warrant officer in charge claimed they had forgotten some of their discipline and that the drill had gone well. My assessment of the drill was somewhat different. When they received an order, the soldiers jumped like automatons. Then they marched away singing, "*Wir marschieren gegen Engeland*!" (We march against England!) They sounded like idiots — particularly considering the state of the war!

A certain German soldier often visits Michelina. Not understanding what he wants, she asks us to translate, so we have gotten to know him, too. He comes to visit us many times, when he is off duty. He is called Emil, from Bielefeld in the Ruhr. He is short and squat, perhaps about 45 years of age and is always speaking of his wife and daughter. He says that Germany has already lost the war and that he, himself, will kill his wife and daughter should the Russians advance as far as Bielefeld. I believe that he suspects who we really are, because he always emphasizes the fact "that for him all people are equal" and "all are human beings."

There was another strafing attack, but this time it was really dangerous. Some ten German vehicles were in the village and just outside the parameter. They were loaded with artillery ammunition and big caliber ones. If only they'd have exploded...

The British fighters dived above our heads, turned with their wings and then came down one after the other like a chain, shooting and sowing small bombs. I stayed near a window and could see a group of Nazis, who seem amused watching the whole scene. Suddenly I saw them shout — running to take cover behind a wall, yelling at me — "Get inside!" Over the roof a fighter plane appeared at top speed, releasing a dozen cannon shots, then climbed to gain altitude…and a terrible explosion rocked the vicinity. The air around us was sucked out as a German truck filled with artillery shells took a direct hit — literally blown up in thin air! The fighter-bombers seemed to have finished their mission and left.

Later I went to have a look at the place where the explosion had taken place. It was pure luck that it happened in the open, on the main road. Had the target been one of the trucks hidden in the square, half the village would have been blown up. Nothing was left on the spot — only a big black stain on the road. And in the middle of the stain was a book — the only "survivor" — with only the corner a little burned. I picked it up and, while leafing through it, an illustrated postcard fell out — maybe a postcard belonging to the soldier who was sitting in the truck, from his wife in Germany. It's a mystery to me how this book didn't disappear in the explosion. I took the book to George, who some time ago decided to start a collection of war souvenirs. He has a half-burned Nazi flag taken from a destroyed vehicle.

The hill of Navelli and the upper levels of the village are literally peppered by pieces of shrapnel from the exploded shells and little bits of truck blown in all directions. During the attack, the butcher Settimio wanted to have a look at what was going on and while opening the door of his balcony, a big piece of shrapnel passed literally between his legs — red and white with the heat of the explosion. He later weighed it and found the shrapnel was a good half-kilo! Enough to kill ten elephants...

The weather is still overcast all the time. It is so gray that you feel depressed and gloomy. This is even worse in light of the uncertainly and danger we sense around us now. Father is more and more nervous and worried.

One day, we drove to a mill outside Aquila with Heinz and the Russian to load flour. We parked at a German sentry post below Aquila, beyond the railway station near a building with a sign that said: "National Shooting Range." It was quite a gloomy place, near a hill surrounded by some potato fields.

In the evening, around 7 p.m., I was called to the command post office by Captain Ehrig. I was stopped in the square by a man in civilian clothes, who asked me in Italian where I was going: there was a curfew. I answered that here the curfew starts at 8 p.m. He told me — in German — to proceed. In German and a civilian?

Five minutes later, I saw the same man arrive at the command post. He was dressed in a black suit. He had cold and piercing eyes and a bullet scar on his chin — I don't remember if it was on the right or the left side — but he behaved like a master, even with Captain Ehrig. There was an officer from the *Wehrmacht* with him — tall and blond, with a bandage and sticking plaster around his neck. Over his left pocket of his uniform he was wearing a S.D. shield (*Sicherheitsdienst*). Everybody was very serious and tense. Captain Ehrig was sitting silently with his head leaning on one hand, studying the floor. Then they brought in a handcuffed Italian whom I had never seen before. I slowly comprehended that this civilian had been apprehended by the Gestapo. The officers of the security service were having lunch at Settimio's when this Italian suddenly appeared, then ran away the moment he saw them, but they had caught him.

This Gestapo man gave me a suspicious look. I feared he was going to ask me something. He mumbled something to Ehrig, and then started interrogating this unlucky Italian. He shouted at him and asked questions while Ehrig and Peters studied their feet. My fear mounted.

The Gestapo man wanted to know why the Italian had fled. He interrogated the fellow in Italian, and then translated into German for the officer and the other two officers. He wanted to hear details that perhaps the Italian didn't know about at all — about partisans and so forth. His papers were not in order. Captain Ehrig showed me his documents, but I told him I didn't know anything about identity papers. But the man under interrogation showed no fear: he had a little black beard and wore some kind of battledress — deep blue, like a sailor's jacket — and his composure was serene. The Gestapo man went on questioning him without respite. Glancing sideways I could see Berber leaning on the opposite wall, watching me intently — perhaps to see how I would react. I wondered what this man wanted from me. I didn't believe he knew what Captain Ehrig knows about me. I tried to remain calm; it was quite impossible. I feared I would be interrogated next, and I was truly terrorized by the thought. He looked at me from time to time — his looks were inquisitive and bone chilling — and I could hardly bear the suspense. At last Captain Ehrig took me aside, led me out of the room and said, "There's no need for you to be here any longer. You can leave now. Thank you."

I retold this story at home and to the "gang" — making quite an impression. That very evening, while listening to the radio, we took pleasure in hearing of the big aerial bombing of Berlin; while in Italy the Allies were crossing the Rapido River, east of Cassino. Already a whole week, to cross the Rapido... It can't be as wide as the Atlantic!?

The next morning, totally by chance, I saw MPs putting the handcuffed Italian in a car and driving away. The Gestapo man disappeared, too.

There was a new air attack on the road near Civitaretenga. I observed the show from the square, mixed in with Nazi soldiers. I was amused by their running commentary of the action: whenever a fighter dived, they shouted, amused. When there was the roar of an explosion, they cursed. And when the airplane flew low over the square, they ran to hide behind the trees in order not to be seen. Strafing every vehicle, even motorcycles, the Allies by their total mastery of the air have compelled the Nazis to move their convoys only by night — wearing down the drivers and slowing down movement to a crawl because the trucks have to drive without headlights. Of course for us, because our house is located along the main road, it is very difficult to sleep at night with all the noise from the road. And when armored-tracked vehicles pass by, the entire house trembles.

Emil told us that should the British approach Navelli, all the Italian children and youngsters would be deported to Russia — that this had already happened in southern Italy, where a shipload of Italian children was deported to Russia. But by the tone of his voice, he didn't sound very convinced by his own story.

One evening we listened to a broadcast from Bari. I heard the "international" news for the first time in my life in a program of the workers' party. I was impressed. Aurelio was pleased.

At the command post, Captain Ehrig told us he was going on leave to Germany until some time after New Year's Eve, that Captain Corn was going back to the front line, and that Lieutenant Peters would now be in charge! We were now really in "good hands"… The Captain wanted to take leave from my father, too. Father was worried because Peters the Nazi is now taking over, and told me to be very careful. He himself is not going near the command post anymore. And I will have to pay attention carefully to every word I say to paratrooper Peters.

On the last day of November, Captain Ehrig left for Germany.

DECEMBER 1943

Listening to the radio in the evening, I heard that the

"Italian Social Republic" (Mussolini's state) has declared all Jews to be enemies of the state and they are to be put in concentration camps. We are very worried, but equally determined not to get caught.

In the morning, a very frightened Mr. Degen visited us. He told us that he heard in an Allied radio broadcast he listened to at Adolfo's house that the Jews in Italy are being advised to try to escape deportation to Poland by all means, and he was very scared. We tried to calm him down. We told him that he must have misunderstood — thinking he'd heard "Polonia" instead of "Bologna." He left perhaps a little convinced — but *we* know it must be Poland because it is now two years since my grandmother and one of mother's brothers were deported to Poland, and we have had no word about what became of them since.

With a somewhat heavy heart, I went for my first day under the command of Lieutenant Peters, but he behaved well. Most of the work was left to the clerk, and Peters merely looked on with his characteristic sarcastic and ironical smile. Advocate Santucci sat by his side and both spoke French. I believe that Santucci came to help ease things for me a bit. They talked in French, which I did not understand, so instead I listened to the radio, which was playing some German military music, and then the daily communication from Hitler's headquarters with the news. Lieutenant Peters' face clouded over, because the Russian were advancing. That is, the radio was saying that the Germans have redeployed to "shorten their lines," but I believe Peters understood perfectly well the meaning of "shortening."

The local secretary and the flat-footed mayor arrived. They had been summoned. What was happening? The Lieutenant declared that in the month of December — precisely on the 24th, or Christmas Eve — the soldiers in the fighting line must get better food. To do this, the town council must deliver the wheat still in the central store, so cakes could be baked for the soldiers of the Reich "who fight to keep the war far away from Navelli." He told them jokingly that, "if they do not comply, he will hang them" — closing his own fingers around his neck for dramatic impact. Clearly, he was letting us know that he is empowered to do so, and expects no argument. They got the message. Did they have any choice?

One afternoon, while on my way to George's house for one of our usual meetings, I encountered Lieutenant Peters. He put one hand on my shoulder (I am taller then him) and ordered me to find out why the local donkeys bray — *i-a-i-a*. I gave him a confused look — not sure what he was driving at. When I told this to the "gang," they laughed. They told me to tell Peters that the donkeys heehaw like this only when they see him! Of course I decided not give him this answer.

When I met him again, I told him I didn't know the answer. He started to laugh, and retorted, "They do it because they are donkeys!" I could have punched him in the face.

We still have bad weather, very bad indeed. This is saddening because even the Allied planes don't show themselves in this weather.

Emil visits us almost every evening, for hours. From

time to time he brings us a present — loaves of bread, black German army bread, which is very tasty when it's fresh. This bread is a true boon, as our resources are dwindling. It's impossible to take care of everything solely on what my father earns from his lessons.

Emil says that sometimes he sees me in the evening (when I return from listening to the radio about 10:30 p.m.). He says that if he stands guard, I will be able to pass even after curfew because he doesn't care.

One afternoon, after returning with Heinz from a trip to Aquila, I couldn't find anybody at George Osmo-Morris's house. I believed I knew where everybody had gone. I walked out of the village in the direction of the "Donkeys' Paradise" ravine. Of course, I took precautions that nobody would spot me. After a quick descent among wet rocks and muddy projections, I reached the cave. There, unseen by anybody, and invisible from above, I found Aurelio, George, Ugo, Pierino, Giuseppino and Luigi oiling the weapons, dismantling them and then reassembling them — making sure the bolts worked smoothly. After another half hour, we all left. I think Aurelio is planning something, but since he says nothing, it's better not to ask.

At the German command post, it's always the same routine. Whenever Peters meets the town mayor and De Guido the secretary, he puts his hand around his neck, and they smile uneasily. But they do deliver the wheat, and the farmers continue to deliver their weekly cup of oil and one onion.

Peters was talking with Advocate Santucci. He asked Santucci how old I was. He really didn't believe I was going on sixteen. Judging from my height, he though I must have been nineteen or twenty. But Santucci convinced him of my true age. Nobody else entered the office, and the conversation went on. Peters commented on my knowledge of German. He told us that many times he had to laugh because I didn't know where to put the verbs, but added that this was natural for an Italian — concluding that all in all, I still spoke the language quite well, in spite of my grammatical mistakes.

Santucci had a terrible idea of talking to Peters about my drawings. (I ignore how *he* knows about them.) Lieutenant Peters was very curious, and asked if I might show them to him some day. Then everybody left, and I went to listen to the radio.

Traveling with Heinz and the warrant officer of the bakery ovens, we reached S. Demetrio — some 15 kilometers from Navelli in the direction of Aquila: a nice, big, quiet place with a German hospital full of wounded soldiers and a field-based slaughterhouse where I saw Negroes in British uniform doing some work. They must have been POWs, but from the smiles on their faces, they seemed to be faring okay. At least the situation they found themselves in ensured they were well fed. Heinz had been ordered to procure wood for the ovens. In a couple of hours, with the help of Italian workers, many tall and old trees were cut and loaded on the trucks amidst the curses of the Italian farmers, who received no payment in exchange, of course.

The 8th Army is finally attacking — at last! The news on the radio tells us that the British divisions have gone into battle, and although the fighting has been very hard and bloody, they have already established bridgeheads at several places across the Sangro River. We are very happy. The Sangro is not far away, and we hope against hope that the Allies will go around the Majella and reach us. Let's hope.

By chance I was present when the Nazi soldiers received a lesson on how to use the Italian light machine gun — the same type the "gang" has. I even dismantle and reassemble it once, and do it quite well. For the last two evenings, Aurelio and five other boys from the "gang" (I only know one of them, Luigi Alterio) patrolled the main road, from 6–9 p.m., in the direction of Capestrano — armed. But as fate would have it, no German convoys passed by, so they had to return to the cave and conceal the weapons, again. They decided to return to the main road, again, the next evening.

The British have managed to hold the bridgeheads across the Sangro, despite bloody fighting. One bridgehead is near Lanciano, the other one below S. Vito Chietino, near the mouth of the river. We tensely follow the news on the radio, but the offensive is only a few days old and the terrain is very difficult, with the German "winter line" resisting fiercely. At home, Father is somewhat skeptical about this offensive. So am I, but we must keep our hopes high.

German traffic on the main road is more intense now. This is natural. When the battle line is active, one has to supply it, and convoy after convoy travel noisily past our door, pushing through the mud and the rain and the cold, to bring up supplies. Because of the bad weather, there are almost no Allied planes in the air. What a pity!

When the British airplanes do come over, they first have to cross the line of anti-aircraft fire in Popoli as well as the surrounding hills. So, almost daily, we are treated, sometimes for hours, to a concert of guns. Steadily the air is split by gunfire, and in the sky we can see a barrier of small black clouds forming, among which Allied airplanes leap forward agilely, always getting through unscathed. The problem is that the shrapnel from the shells rains down on our heads and it is safest to watch this "show" from behind a window.

I made a selection of my best drawings. (I am drawing a lot now, since I have so many interesting scenes unfolding right here before my very eyes.) I brought them to Lieutenant Peters, who looked at them together with Advocate Santucci. Peters likes the big drawing — a watercolor portraying a Napoleonic battle. I believed he was hinting how *much* he liked it, but I closed my ears.

He got the wheat. Now he wants the entire stock of almonds nuts. He wants the soldiers on the battle line to eat *mandelkuchen* with almonds for Christmas…and he wants men and women to crack open the almonds, as well. Of course, he gets everything he wants. After all, he gave orders to break the locks on the storehouse before asking for delivery of their stores. He asks for permission only as a formality. The actual commandeering of the stores is carried out by Peters and his soldiers.

Through some very able work of "persuasion and propaganda," over the past few months the "gang" have managed to enlist some young men from Civitaretenga, but I don't know if they actually know everything about the weapons. Discussions are restricted — limited to general talk and ideas. The meetings are held, of course, employing passwords. We meet on Sundays, in an abandoned and half-ruined house among a little forest of oak trees, between the graveyard and the hill where Civitaretenga sits.

8 DECEMBER 1943

Last night was the big moment for the "gang" — their "baptism of fire." They did not want to take me along because of my age and because they believe I would be more useful staying close to the German command, to see what may happen.

Aurelio and six others, all armed, positioned themselves in the evening on one of the bends of the road to Capestrano, Aurelio among the bushes, and the rest with a light machine gun behind a little wall along the road. As Aurelio related, they were all very keyed up. At about 8 p.m., a German convoy started to pass them. Aurelio was the first to open fire. He jumped out of the bushes, stood and fired all the bullets in his handgun at the lead car. The Germans stopped and jumped out of the car running down onto the rocks. According to the plan, at the same moment, the machinegun was supposed to open fire, too. Luigi Alterio was holding it. But after only one shot, the weapon jammed. From the other cars and trucks, Germans opened fire and bullets began to fly in every direction. Aurelio was left with no ammunition. With the machine gun jammed, and hearing no automatic fire, the other five, armed with rifles, lost their courage and ran down into the ravine followed by a hail of bullets — at least not forgetting to take their weapons with them. Aurelio left last. So, the first action was a failure because of the machine gun.

Nevertheless, the impression left on the village the next morning by the attack was tremendous. Nobody knew who did it and everybody feared some beastly retaliation.

In the afternoon I went, curious and fearful, to the command post. After all, I have to observe the reactions of the Germans very carefully, and report them to the "gang." Lieutenant Peters was really furious — shouting and raving, he called the *Carabinieri* commander, the town secretary and the town mayor and threatened to take three hostages from Navelli and three hostages from Capestrano, since the incident took place between the two villages. Then, angrily, he sent me away.

I related all this at George's house. Everybody was very uptight. Only Aurelio kept his cool. Despite being quite small, he is very courageous. In the evening, we went to a meeting with the people of Civitaretenga. We reached the little house and waited for about twenty minutes, but nobody arrived. Aurelio cursed them, calling them cowards. Now that a decisive step had been taken, they feared to be seen. Aurelio sent everyone home. He and I made a long detour across the stony hills behind Navelli where the weapons had been stashed because nobody had time to take them back to the cave. They were still hidden. He will take care of returning them later to the cave.

The whole village is still on alert. So are we. Peters was holding sessions with his officers, and we overheard (I am not admitted to those sessions, of course) that he gave the order to take three hostages in Capestrano. Here in Navelli, however, no one was taken. We also heard that in the car attacked there was a woman who was killed. Aurelio shrugged; really nobody had thought about it.

It is a week since the British 8th Army began its attack, and the fighting must be very hard because the advance is minor, and the results, too. But it seems that the Germans feel very threatened, because the movement of the supply convoys to the frontline, creeping in our direction, leave a big impression. A never-ending chain of vehicles and men pass before our eyes, in the cold and rain and mud, aboard motorized units. The faces of the Nazis are hard and tired. They cannot sleep by night and are traveling towards death. The artillery, the soldiers and the ammunition move along, destined towards the front line which is not far away from us — perhaps 25-30 minutes by car to the south.

I have almost no contact with the soldiers of the bakery unit. They know me but don't talk to me. I have only had some words with a couple of them. One once asked me where he could find stamps for his collection. Another, a Viennese clerk working with the engines and responsible for delivery of the bread, stopped me one day and showed me his neck, asking me if I could "see something." I couldn't see anything, but he told me that a doctor told him

67

he was developing a goiter. I personally really couldn't have cared less...

Emil has visited us at our home several times, but when I return home from listening to the radio at about 9 p.m., he is no longer on sentry duty because he's working nights. The curfew now starts at 7 p.m., but I return home only at 9. Instead of walking where the sentries are posted, I cross the muddy fields. My shoes respond by falling to pieces. My feet are always cold and frozen. Miss Quintilio really pities me, but I'm always quite content with my lot, despite the hardships. My family is in arduous shape. Livio, too, is without shoes, and almost never leaves home. He always lights the fire in the kitchen and helps Mother with whatever he can. Father is very worried and pessimistic. But we all hope this offensive may help us.

We were very tense about the radio and the Germans. Lieutenant Peters released the three hostages in Capestrano, but he was still angry, and I was afraid to go to the German command post. For a few days I managed to stay away. We heard good news on the radio: the British have entered Lanciano and S. Vito Chietino and advanced a few hundred yards under heavy fighting and very bad weather conditions. On the mountains around us there have already been heavy snowfalls.

One evening, after leaving the Quintilo house with Aurelio, we stopped to observe a new kind of spectacle: around the tops of the faraway mountains, clearly visible on a dark night, we could see flashes — many flashes together with thunder-like noises: the front line! The night sky was lit by a reddish-blue flash and culminated in a rumbling noise. We were both really happy. Not only could we hear the battle line, we could now even see it! And for a short moment, we were able to forget the worries of the last days and enjoy this sight of liberation approaching.

Lieutenant Peters called me to ask why I hadn't shown up in the last few days. He had already asked my father the same question, adding that he missed me. This I can live without! He asked me if, by any chance, I was afraid of him, or maybe I feared he would charge me with some connection with the December 8th attack, or could be arrested as a hostage. Then he started to laugh, and told me that in his opinion the attack was carried out by escaped British POWs who had formed a gang. Anyway, he promised that the area would be combed thoroughly, again and again.

Later on, the daily routine of farmers arriving to request permits, complain or ask for advice resumed. The main road is still choked by Nazi convoys, going up or down in the mud, under heavy rains.

I have noticed that one of the main characteristics of war, so far, is that everyone curses and swears all the time. It looks as if whole armored convoys or whole units of soldiers are propelled forward only on the force of their cursing. But it is really quite normal that these men — reduced to living and acting like beasts or machines, deprived of sleep and sent into battle, swear and curse at everything and everybody. Everything and every one of them has become part of the movement of a big machine that can be observed now in the midst of a great battle being fought to our south – a battle we hope will soon bring our liberation.

Because of the heavy traffic, we always have "unwanted guests" in our place. They are soldiers who have reached their limits and have stopped for a few hours to regain their strength. They appear by day and by night. They come in, kicking open the door with their feet. They don't ask for anything. They merely take any chair they can find and sit down. They are all tired, dirty and unshaven. They swear and curse, and we surreptitiously listen. They don't know we understand them. They curse everything — Hitler and Germany, the war and Italy. They are discontented with everything, yet when they receive orders to move out — orders that spell more strain and fatigue and the battle ahead — they jump to attention, become machines again and move on. By night, these "uninvited visitors" are a genuine plague. They go into the farmers' houses — gun in one hand, flashlight in the other — and take over the beds. In the morning they depart — sometimes with the bed sheets. The soldiers of the field bakery try to protect the village somehow. Yesterday *Feldwebel* Heinz arrived at our house by chance, and saw a group of Bavarian soldiers in our kitchen putting some mattresses on the floor. Shouting, he chased them out. But after he left, they simply returned to our kitchen.

Peters, it seems, does not know what to do. He sent a report to headquarters in Aquila about the "bandits'" attack. I told this to Aurelio and George, and we decided to act. This time I was to participate, too. We needed to transfer the weapons from the ravine because the Germans could start combing the area around the site of the ambush. In the evening, we met near the old fountain and, under the cover of darkness, descended into the rift. It is difficult enough to go down there by day. By night it is crazy. But we did it anyway. Then, for more than two hours — we were all there — we worked like madmen, carrying bundles of rifles, sub-machine guns and the heavy automatic weapons up the ravine to where the donkeys were waiting with somebody, just near the road where German convoys pass. But there was no other way. The most heavy and dangerous work was handling the ammunition boxes and the two canisters of hand grenades. We made several trips towards Navelli, concealing the weapons in a cave-stable near the edge of the village, on the slopes of a hill. By 9 p.m., we are already safely back — sitting next to the radio, as usual. In the evening, when there is neither fog nor low clouds and I look out, I can always see those flashes on the mountains. The noise of the guns is muffled by the noise of traffic on the road. The very heavy fighting going on to our south is reflected on the faces of the German soldiers passing through — dirty, tired faces that reflect the terror of war and battle.

When they talk, they say the British artillery fire is much worse than the gunfire at Stalingrad. So they say. Emil always brings us bread. Now that he works night shifts, he manages to make quick visits to our house, which is very near to the bakeries, to bring us fresh-baked bread.

Lieutenant Peters' ordered the ovens to be put into the big sports building where the Russians are lodged, because of the bad weather and cold. The owners of the building protested when they saw the gates and doors broken down and holes drilled through the ceiling for the oven chimneys, but there was no use complaining.

In the morning and evening at George's home everybody played cards — clearly in order to try and overcome our anxiety — and George Osmo-Morris won a pile of lira. I don't like cards, so I sat in a broken-down armchair near the fireplace warming my feet.

For the time being, the life of the other "interned people" goes on quietly. Everybody is busy finding food, but the farmers are reluctant to sell anything. They fear the winter and the approaching war, and hide whatever food they have in their cellars. Billig never leaves home. Degen comes out from time to time. The Osmo-Morrises keep up their quarrels. Their little dog Lilla has become terrorized by the explosions, and now starts to tremble if she hears even the *sound* of aircraft. The dog understands the connection between the noise of the planes flying over our heads and the explosions that follow. Clever dog.

One night, on orders from Peters, two soldiers woke me up at about 1 a.m. It was freezing outside. What was happening? The daughter of Baron Francesconi was having a baby, and I had to help the Germans phone the hospital in Aquila for an ambulance.

Peters said he was unable to free a car, even if she was in mortal danger. Doctor Falconio was with me, and he swore and cursed the officer. After the phone call, we waited for the ambulance from Aquila to come — if they found enough gas for the journey. The night was calm and clear. From the Majella, clear and high even by night, right in front of our noses, came an unbroken rumble, like a big thunderstorm. Doctor Falconio naively asked the paratrooper guarding us with his rifle what the noise could be. The soldier answered, "The front line," and then said to me, "Please tell the doctor that you do not mention the hangman's rope in the house of a condemned man." An hour later, the ambulance arrived from Aquila.

The next morning I met Peters, who told me that guns would shortly be deployed in Navelli, and I should not be afraid when they start shooting. Soon afterward, the guns arrived. One of them took up a position near our house. Our landlady was very scared. They were 88-mm.[13] pieces, mounted on trucks but, to our great relief, they left two hours later.

Trenches are now being dug in Navelli — one around the villa Francesconi in order to protect the crossroads, and another to the west of our house at the entrance to the village. Thirty Italian workers are digging the trenches in the mud and in the rain.

At the lessons with Giosi, Father talked more about the fighting than about German grammar. The 8th Army has already advanced some 20 kilometers, reaching Tollo, near Chieti and Guardiagrele in our area, and has started climbing up the slopes of the Majella. In the evening, the sky was violet with artillery flashes.

The Allied broadcasting stations, especially "Radio Bari," continue to advise the Jews to escape from the

13 The German 88-mm. gun is an anti-aircraft artillery piece from World War II.

Nazis and the fascists, and urge the Italians to help hide Jews. We were terrified to learn that the interned Jews in Capestrano, seven kilometers from us, had been arrested by the S.S. and taken away.

Convoys block the roads day and night. Everything is thrown into the battle. We watch the spectacle with interest. Today, the clouds have thinned out a bit, and British wings are over our heads once more — sinking their teeth into the Germans. These air raids are always anounced by the German anti-aircraft guns in Popoli, five or six kilometers to the south of Navelli as the crow flies. But the aircraft get through, skimming the ground and the treetops, firing with all their weapons and attacking the roads. I observed an attack from a window in George's house. Here in the village on the top of the hill, we are higher than the aircraft and can see everything from above. After the attack, we went down to the road. There was a dead man lying there, killed by shrapnel and the blast. He lay on the grass, his face to the sky, with sheep grazing all around him. It seemed very strange how a body of a man lying there like that looked smaller than in reality. Underneath him the grass was full of blood. I lifted the cloth covering his face and saw it contorted in a grin, eyes open wide, while the sheep continued to munch the wet December grass, unconscious that death had just passed through in a burst of fire and flames.

The "gang" — I don't know how — got wind of the existence of other partisan groups on the Majella and in some places around the Gran Sasso that are much more efficient than we. Aurelio would like to make contact with them, but nobody knows how.

Lieutenant Peters received some orders at last from Aquila. He was told to put a big sign on the road just outside Navelli warning German motor traffic of the danger of guerrilla warfare in the area between Navelli and Caporciano.

As always, there was music on the radio, but this time it was not military music but jazz, and the woman spoke English. Peters asked me suddenly if I understood and spoke English. I do understand the language quite well, but I replied that I didn't even know what in language the announcer was speaking.

I made a trip to Aquila with Peters and the bakery warrant officer. They bought paper bags for the sweets to be sent to the troops for Christmas. We passed through S. Elia, still smoking after the air attack yesterday morning. The attack was quite pointless as there were no bridges, road crossings or Nazi forces there. The little hamlet had been reduced to a complete heap of rubble. Coming back again, between S. Elia and Paganica, there were fighter-bombers overhead! Peters stopped the car and hid it under some trees. We waited for about 20 minutes. When the danger had passed, we returned to Navelli.

Now there is a nice sign in German posted near the old spring, near a dozen other road signs, saying: "ACHTUNG BANDENGEFAHR!" — "Beware of Bandits!" Aurelio laughed when I translated it for him.

The battle to the north of the Sangro River continued, and tanks passed through on Navelli's roads. It was a very long convoy, and the ground shook under their tracks. It was quite a show of strength. They were all very dirty, but their long guns left a big impression. The soldiers in their black overalls with the silver skull surveyed the world around them with stern faces. The farmers were very impressed seeing these steel monsters, but started cursing them when these Panzers turned, broke down a wall and damaged the corner of a house, as if making some kind of joke.

My shoes are now in such a pitiful condition, we decided to give them to the shoemaker to make some wooden soles. It will be great to walk around in the mud and frost with wooden clogs.

It is very cold by night. Our bedroom is freezing when we go to bed, so Father, Mother and Livio warm some blocks in the fireplace and wrap them up in paper to take to bed to warm the sheets. I don't use them because for some reason I warm up quickly without any bricks.

Every kind of Nazi soldier continues to enter our house, as they do all the other houses along the main road, wishing to warm up a bit and rest for a while. They must be very shaken and tired.

In the village to the south where the Nazis are retreating, it seems their Teutonic fury is being unleashed in all its horror. Among the peasants, rumors circulate of killings, whole villages burnt down, and plundering. For the last two days we see Germans on horseback on the main road, moving in the opposite direction from the supply convoys, driving great herds of horses and donkeys forward, all stolen from the farmers. The people of Navelli are terrified. The Nazis are filled with wrath and are taking with them the meager possessions of even the poorest farmers of the Abruzzi mountains. They chase the inhabitants out of their houses in villages soon to be occupied by the British. And all this in deep winter. These refugees fill the roads, too. When the Allies approach, the Germans take the livestock, then give the inhabitants half an hour to leave their homes, plunder the homes and torch the village, and the British find only a heap of rubble.

Michelina is involved with the Nazi soldiers and already has a nice dowry collected from all the presents she receives from them — silverware, linen, kitchen implements — all plundered. From the mountains we hear the rumble of guns.

This evening, while returning from the radio, there was darkness all around. It was cloudy and I could see some German coaches stopping on the road. I looked inside and saw scores of British and Indian POWs with helmets still on their heads, their faces tense, covered from head to foot in mud — the same mud we saw on the German soldiers who passed by and came to rest in our kitchen.

It is always the same at the German command post. Peters looks bored and talks a lot with Advocate Santucci.

At George's place we talked a lot, too. Nothing has happened. We are quite calm. We visited the stable-cave to check on the weapons, and at last we understood why the machinegun jammed; in the intensity of the action, Luigi Alterio forgot to open the breach for the spent cartridges to be ejected so the firing system could not feed new ammunition in from the magazine. We almost drowned Luigi with our curses. We dismantled the weapons, oiled them and noted how they work. Then we buried the ammunition cases and covered them with dirt.

24 December 1943

This morning, before I could wash and dress, a car stopped in front of our house and two Republican fascists dismounted. We followed their moves with mounting worry and fear. They came in and asked for Father. One of them was a commissar from the Aquila political police — the *Questura*[14] — named Mario De Nardis. He asked if we were the Fleischmanns, how many of us were here, how many suitcases we had, and told us we must be ready to be taken away at any time.

Degen and Billig came down in a hurry. Naturally they were as upset as we all were. They decided that the three women — my mother, Miss Degen and Miss Billig — would try to go to Aquila sometime in the next few days. The women would go because the men would face more danger. At Aquila they will go to the *Questura* and try to gather more information so we'll know what to do.

The Englishmen weren't issued any warning. Just the Jews. Every morning, Miss Moldenhower, like a true British philanthropist, prepares coffee and milk for the German sentry posted before the German army office opposite the house where she lives.

I referred the news to my friends, and they assured me they would do everything possible to stop our deportation. Then they departed for church. It was Christmas Eve, and I remained with George Osmo-Morris and Adriana. We talked about different things. We haven't heard anything

14 Police headquarters.

from the Eibenschutz family in Capestrano since their arrest by the S.S. Who knows where they are?

In the evening, Emil brought us bread with some cakes — the same as those sent to the soldiers at the front.

The weather is awful. An icy wind is blowing, and from time to time it rains, and this produces a frozen mud. My so-called "shoes" are ready. The problem is I can't walk any better with these wooden clogs than my previous ones. It feels like I have something under my feet, but I can only walk stiffly because the wood doesn't bend like leather. One has to have patience.

The British army has encountered very tough obstacles but they are now some 30 kilometers nearer, and we all hope they can get through the last few kilometers that separate us. Now it's impossible to hear anything, because the bad weather absorbs the noise of gunfire.

On the road, the Nazis drove herds of horses, donkeys and goats they plundered from the villages to the south, villages they later destroyed. They even left a dozen or so goats with Peters' unit for fresh milk.

A young man riding on a horse took a look around, read the road sign "Navelli," asked something of the farmers and turned towards our house. He was wearing a dirty German uniform and high boots. He dismounted and asked Father and Mother if we were the Fleischmanns. My parents were frightened, but he reassured them — revealing that he too was ... Jewish! His name was Altman and he was interned in Guardiagrele — a village occupied some days ago by the 8th Army. The Germans caught him, dressed him in an old German uniform and forced him to follow them, ordering him to take care of the plundered horses. "*Jude hier! Jude gehe hier!*" (Jew come here, Jew go there!). He could not escape and didn't know where he was headed. He as unable to flee because the soldiers threatened him all the time.

He implored Father to run away. He said that when the British approach, all the interned people are deported or liquidated on the spot. Then, sad and sorry, he mounted his horse and followed the Germans. Who knows where the poor devil will end up?

Mother, Mrs. Degen and Billig left this morning for Aquila, despite the awful weather. A German truck very kindly gave them a lift. They returned frozen in the evening, and told us that the Jews who found refuge in Aquila and the very same commissar — De Nardis — gave them only one piece of advice: escape while you can.

My mother related there were two German soldiers in the car in which they returned. One of them was from Vienna and had quite an open argument with the driver about the situation of Germany. The two tried to convince him that Hitler was a scoundrel and the war was lost. Maybe the two sensed that the three women were Jewish and therefore spoke like that.

Due to the cold weather, I fell ill with the flu, and informed Lieutenant Peters that I wouldn't be able to work for a couple of days.

Father, Billig and Mr. Degen went away for a whole day. They left for a little village called Bominaco far away from the main road and high in the mountains, looking for a possible new place of refuge. But they returned quite discouraged.

George, Ugo and Aurelio paid me a visit, bringing with them news they had heard on the radio: the British suffered quite a setback to the south of Chieti. They had to retreat from Orsogna with heavy losses. The fighting goes on in Ortona and on the Majella, but they are quite pessimistic. They told me that they believe they have found a contact with a partisan group operating in the next valley — a group nobody has heard of. Then they left, wishing me well. I do not like being stuck in bed without being able to get around, see what's happening and listen to the radio. But if I don't rest now I won't get rid of this flu for the whole winter. And with what may lie ahead of us, it's certainly better to be well and ready to meet whatever comes. In bed, I can hear the noise of the German convoys on the road outside — long convoys of horse-drawn columns with huge Belgian horses that elicit admiration among the local villagers.

In the afternoon, I heard the noise of aircraft overhead. I went to have a look from the window and could see two British fighters and one German fighterdog fighting. After about five minutes, the German aircraft suddenly began to lose altitude and, with a high whining whistle, crashed to the ground beyond Civitaretenga. I returned to bed very pleased.

31 December 1943

Father, Livio, Mr. Degen and Mr. Billig left very early in the morning to have a look in another more remote village as a possible hiding place. The place is called Carapelle and is hidden in the mountains. They returned in the evening. Father was very depressed and tired. They made it halfway, but couldn't proceed because of a snowstorm. Billig, with his weak heart, had to stop. In the evening it also started to snow heavily in Navelli. At midnight, we woke up to the sound of heavy rifle fire and automatic weapons. The noise was somewhat weakened by the thickly falling snow. A very heavy snowstorm was raging outside. The Germans were greeting the New Year 1944 by shooting in the air. The Russians were singing and drinking at Michelina's house. What will the New Year of 1944 bring us?

JANUARY 1944

We woke up and rose to a white morning. Perhaps 40 centimeters of snow had fallen during the night. Our old landlord Luigi was able to open the door only with great effort because great quantities of snow, blown by the wind, were heaped up everywhere, and in some places even the road couldn't be crossed. I put on my long trousers and over them I pulled on my shorts (since both are torn anyway). I went out to help my mother carry water from the fountain. Around us, all of nature had changed overnight: everything was white — the fields, the hills, the trees, the houses, the trucks and the tents. It could have been beautiful, had the Nazis not been there!

82

We ran into the soldiers from the ovens. They were swearing. They said that for them, Italy had always meant a country with an eternally blue sky. But the Russians were happy.

A car or some kind of armored vehicle managed to proceed with difficulty. The noise of its engine broke the deep silence blanketing the whole area as long as it was still snowing. We were even unable to hear the rumble of the fighting line. All was silent.

Towards noon I went to George and found everybody there. The snow made everyone cheerful. So were we, but we were panting because climbing the endless steps of Navelli in the snow is something suited for alpine mountain climbers. All the steps and stairs are full of snow and you never know where to put your foot. I had to work even harder with my wooden clogs. In the evening, in order to reach the radio, we literally slipped and slid on our backs. The news disappointed us. They were still fighting in Ortona, but after the setback at Orsogna, the British had ceased all activities — stopping, so to speak, under our noses. The only ones that made us happy were the Russians, who had reached the Polish border and defeated the Nazis all along the line.

In the village square, the German paratroopers were engaging in a very fierce snowball battle, and woe to the Italian who crossed between them! Peters sat at the command post. Everything was nicely warmed up. He told me — laughing sarcastically — that the British would soon be in Pescara.

The village gossip told me of another idiotic gesture

made by old General Santucci: he rose very early in the morning and started shoveling the snow in front of the place where Peters lives, saying: "I have to clean the doorstep so the officer will be able to do his duty!" Peters related this to Captain Corn, here on leave from the front line, and he laughed coarsely. Captain Corn told him about Orsogna, where he had been — how the British were cut off and repulsed and how bravely the British and Indian infantry struggled to cover the retreat from the village. The German "winter line" had not been penetrated, and they were both very delighted.

We now have two new German units in the village: one, at the crossroads, is comprised of soldiers from the military police with the Iron Shield on their tunic (the soldiers call them "*Kettenhunde*" — chain-dogs — because of the iron chain hanging around their neck); the second is a communications platoon — telephone and electrical technicians — living at the last house of the village, some 20 meters from our house. They are an ugly lot — very extreme Nazis.

My mother and the two other ladies had to go to Aquila again, despite the difficult weather, in order to contact two interned sisters — the Metzgers — who know the commissar of the Republican fascist *Questura* De Nardis well, to talk to him about our situation. They took a few kilos of flour with them out of our already dwindling reserves. The policeman needs it because there is nothing to eat in Aquila. A lone German vehicle floundering through the snow agreed to give them a lift and off they went, freezing in the back of the open truck.

Lieutenant Peters called the elders of the town hall. He needed 500 men to shovel the snow and clear the roads for about 10 kilometers around Navelli, and also to dig out the trenches that had filled with snow to the rim. He wanted them the next day.

In the evening, after coming back from listening to the radio (the news told of the fall of Ortona and the stalemate in our area), I found the whole road blocked by armored cars and assault guns. There was complete chaos. At night, all the fighting machines were parked on the side of the road, under a coat of snow, and our kitchen was, as always, choked full with German soldiers around the fireside. On top of all that, outside there was a mass of plundered horses headed north, and they were blocked too, occupying all available stables. They were led by Nazi soldiers who didn't look more than 17 years old — badly equipped and with very low morale.

There was no room for us in the kitchen, so we went up to sleep freezing and on empty stomachs.

Mother came back from Aquila. She told us that she spoke with Mario De Nardis, who repeated again that the only thing to do is to escape — he will try to delay or drag his feet as long as possible to prevent our arrest. He should have done so — arrested us — already in December, but on the pretense of the danger of air attacks he had come only with a small car. That trip was supposed to have served as a warning, for who has ever seen a police officer warning the people he should arrest so long in advance? De Nardis then added that he knew only that

85

we were to be transferred to a place in northern Italy called Fossoli, and from there further on by railway — to a destination he chose to ignore. But with this weather, where could we possibly escape to? Anyway, De Nardis assured us that for the time being, he would not come to take us. Of course we all — and especially Degen and Billig — live under a constant state of impending disaster.

Mr. Giosi promised my father that he would also look for a hiding place. He knows a little village to the south, called S. Benedetto in Perillis, where he could find refuge and be nearer to the front line. But with this weather it is difficult to do anything.

It continued to snow during the night. In the morning, a portion of the parked armored cars departed, but with great difficulty. They worked very hard for a whole hour to start and move each vehicle. The trucks' tires lacked traction on the snow, and instead only made mud. The soldiers cursed and "organized" (stole) cables to put under the wheels. That was how the vehicles finally, and very noisily, departed. One failed and refused to start. It sits just opposite our window. In the morning, the crew of this armored car, having slept inside that iron box, barely managed to emerge from it as the weight of the snow pressed down on the hatch. Now it simply stands there, unable to move.

Lieutenant Peters thinks that the time to shovel aside the snow is premature, because it is still snowing heavily. Anyway, a Nazi snowplow has already done some of the job. As usual, Emil visited us with the usual loaf of bread under his arm. One crew member of the stranded armored car saw him entering the house and went with him. He was thin, with a small black mustache and a little dog — Strupi — who followed him. He was from Berlin and talked about the catastrophic air bombings the Allies have inflicted on his city. He said that the Germans would not be able to go on for long with such a life, and would ultimately collapse.

It is really beautiful — sun and snow. The sky has cleared up completely and is now blue, and the whole landscape around us is white with 40 cm. of snow. With the sun shining, the snow takes on blue shadows. It is a very nice spectacle — this mixture of war and snow. The vehicles — all colored khaki or iron-gray — crisscross the snow, leaving a trail of muddy tracks, and the blue and gray field uniforms and guns are cast in relief against the sun and the white snow. It is interesting to observe the hundreds of Italians working in the snow: Peters walks up and down the road, with his hobnailed boots noisily crunching the snow, swearing like a trooper. The Italians shovel the snow for five minutes, then stick their spades into the ground, laugh, warm up and have a smoke. It is a way of showing some kind of passive resistance. Nobody can say they are not working and nobody can say they are sabotaging the work. It seems that the heaps of snow in the middle of the road are growing instead of lessening, and the Germans are cursing.

Of course, with the sun shining, British aircraft have appeared as well, easily picking up the brown or gray cars moving on the snow.

5 JANUARY 1944

Today the students from the "gang" and I had to do our shift of work. We took spades and shovels, and were taken to shovel snow out of the trenches. The spades were quite heavy, even if you were only shoveling snow. The trenches were deep and the Germans laughed seeing us work. I was very cold and gulped down half a bottle of wine to warm myself up, but I got quite tipsy and fell down into the snow-filled trench. Everybody around me had a good laugh. We worked until dark quite cheerfully. In the evening, we listened to the radio.

Today, after resting from yesterday's work, I went to the Billigs' to pay a visit, but on the way I saw Lieutenant Umbertino skiing on the hill. He is the second-in-command of the "gang" because of his skill in handling weapons. He gave me his skis, and for more than three hours I tried to learn how to use them, but to no avail: all I managed to do was fall over.

Towards the evening, British fighter-bombers appeared. They had discovered a German ammunition convoy limping through the snow. The strafing went on for about an hour between Civitaretenga and S. Pio, eight kilometers to the north, and I could see everything from the top of the hill. Within a short time, 18 trucks were hit and set ablaze, and all the ammunition was blown up. Long into the night we could hear violent explosions, as cases filled with shells and other ammunition exploded with a piercing din.

I must go to Aquila to try and find some place where we can eventually live — abandon Navelli, and try to hide in the town. Miss Quintilo gave me the address of one of her friends who lives on S. Flaviano Street. I will try to get a lift on a long artillery convoy that has stopped here, go there, and leave again tomorrow.

6 JANUARY 1944

At the end of the day, I took off with the convoy. The officer in charge gave me permission to go with them. I found a place on a little truck full of ammunition, and we started out. Near S. Pio, I met Ugo Marrano walking back from Aquila (40 km.), where he had been to investigate whether there was a way to contact the partisans on the Gran Sasso. He greeted me, gesturing wildly with his hands.

Without headlights, the artillery convoys traveled very slowly, and I felt drowsy. After traveling two hours we were only three kilometers from the city. I had to leave my lift, because the Germans turned at the crossroads in the direction of Avezzano.

While I was walking the last three kilometers to Aquila, a fascist militiaman patrolling the road stopped me. I feared he would take me to the *Questura*, but for the remaining half hour of my walk, I managed to talk all the time, babbling a lot of nonsense so that in the end, near Corso in Aquila, he just let me go.

I was in Aquila for two days, but achieved nothing. There was nothing to do there. The only positive thing

I did was buy two newspapers with reports about the Verona trials against Ciano and his accomplices. In the evening — realizing that there was no way of finding any transportation to return home — I simply asked the German military police to help me, telling them I was the interpreter at L. 21063. They put me on a truck full of artillery shells and at about 9 p.m. I was back in Navelli — with nothing accomplished.

When I entered the house, my Father met me. He had been very worried about me for the last two days. We went into the kitchen, where two German soldiers were sitting at the table having dinner. Father asked me for news of the war and, somewhat embarrassed, I answered, "Here, I have brought newspapers with me." But Father laughed and so did the Germans. He told me I was free to talk. They knew who we were.

The story goes like this. In the morning, while Mother was going to fetch water, she heard two German soldiers calling, "Good morning, Mrs. Fleischmann." They were the two soldiers who had been talking badly about Hitler when Mother and the other ladies were coming back from Aquila on the truck. One of them, the short one with the small mustache, was from Vienna. His name was Karl Loher. The other one was a German from Erfurt called Fiegler. They were half-deserters. Fiegler, the older one, had spent two years before the war as an inmate at Dachau as a political anti-Nazi prisoner, and his army paybook bears a stamp saying "politically suspicious." They move around from village to village because they refuse to go to the front line. Loher even told us he was ready to desert, and that he had even made some kind of contact with the "underground," but added, in a very low voice, that he did not completely trust his companion: even if he had been in Dachau, Fiegler was a German, while he — Loher — was an Austrian. They talked the whole evening, after the meager meal we all took together. They had already been at our house for two days and wanted to move on in the morning. They spoke of the morale of the soldiers. Everyone was fed up and the whole situation couldn't last too much longer. They asked me if by chance I knew somebody ready to buy their uniforms and...guns! Then we went to sleep.

The next morning, I told Aurelio of the possibility of buying two rifles, and taking two German deserters into the "gang." But when we reached our house, we found out that these two desperate people had already departed.

The front line is flashing, but does not move. The snow is beginning to freeze. Over the last days it has snowed intermittently. The bread we get from Emil is now a real necessity. At the German command post there is very little to do. The unit is to leave in a couple of days, after nearly three months in Navelli. Lieutenant Peters is absent most of the time. He is always traveling about. Some of the field bakery ovens have already been dismantled and taken away.

I reported this news to the group at George's house. The house now looks like an "iron-clad" shack with all the war "souvenirs" he has collected. Some of the group wanted to act immediately, but Aurelio and George were reluctant to do anything against L.21063 because of the risk of terrible reprisals in the wake of any action. Somebody proposed to free some of the Russian prisoners, but someone else objected — arguing that it would only amount to additional mouths to feed.

Lieutenant Peters met with the town council and notified them that his unit was leaving Navelli. He handed them a paper testifying that "Navelli behaved loyally and decently toward the German troops stationed there."

Father fears that Peters might "kidnap" me and take me away as an interpreter. He told me that in the coming days, when the Germans leave, I should stay away from the command post. But I didn't believe it.

16 JANUARY 1944

The whole village is in turmoil. Two Russians have escaped. When I crossed the square, *Feldwebel* Heinz and another German — both very agitated and with guns in their hands — stopped me and ordered me to follow them to look for the Russians. Armed Germans entered all the houses to search the premises and threatened everyone. The farmers were frightened, and begged me to explain to the furious Nazis that they didn't know anything about the two escaped Russian POWs. We searched the village in every direction, and Heinz — "reading" my behavior — understood what I was thinking, but didn't say a word. We reached the eastern part of the village, nicknamed "Siberia" because of the cold winds that blow from this side. It is here in one of the last stable-caves where the weapons are stashed… While we were searching one of the houses we heard shots and shouting. Two Germans had discovered one of the Russians inside the cave that held the weapons!

I held my breath as the two Nazis shot at the lock and opened the door. One came back with the Russian — Alex the cook. Thank heavens: while searching the cave, he didn't discover the weapons. The other one, with a whip in his hand, hit the Russian in the face, shouting, until he broke his whip over the prisoner's head. The Italians standing around and observing this barely managed to restrain themselves from hitting the German. Heinz continued to search for another hour and then, very distractedly, told me to go.

In the evening, Aurelio told me the second Russian was safe, hiding near a little wood around Civitaretenga.

Later, when I returned home, the kitchen was occupied of course, this time by two Bavarian soldiers who had little desire to reach the front line and therefore had put their own car temporarily "out of commission."

17 JANUARY 1944

The Germans searching the houses have arrested one member of the "gang" who helped the POW escape. They found some personal effects of the escaped prisoners in his house. His name is Torlone. The man left in charge in

Navelli, for the moment, is *Feldwebel* Heinz, and Father went to speak with him to ask him to free Torlone. At first Heinz refused, talking about the "laws of war," but Father argued, diplomatically, that with the unit now leaving Navelli, it would be a shame at this point to destroy the amiable relationship of the past three months between the Germans and Italians. In the end Heinz agreed and, in the evening, with the Germans' departure, Torlone was freed.

Coming back from the radio late in the evening, I found, much to my great surprise, three pairs of new mountain boots on the kitchen table! The two Bavarian soldiers had sold Father three pairs of boots that they must have looted somewhere else. I threw away my wooden clogs and noticed that the new boots were three sizes bigger than my foot, but it didn't matter. Father had used our last 750 lire to buy them (at 250 lire a pair). Almost nothing!

The next day, Father managed to sell one pair to a farmer for 1,200 lire. Thus we made quite a tidy profit plus gained two pairs of boots — one for me and one for Livio. How different I feel walking in the snow and mud with these huge new boots!

The only ones left in the village are the signal unit soldiers. The soldiers from the military police called me to help them with a few unimportant things and that was all. Now my days pass much more pleasantly — at George's house or listening to the radio broadcasts. I even asked the MPs for a circulation permit after curfew.

One day we saw a very interesting spectacle: from the

direction of the British lines we could see something like a balloon rising into the sky and coming in our direction. Then, it slowly returned. Not even the German soldiers from the signal unit who use field glasses were able to figure out what it meant.

22 JANUARY 1944

The Allies have landed at Anzio-Nettuno. I ran home to relate the good news, very happy. Perhaps this action will change the general situation a little. At George's house I learned that Aurelio and George had succeeded in making contact with the leader of a partisan group, who asked them for some assistance. He will try to obtain some explosives, essential for sabotage.

24 JANUARY 1944

We are in for a very "hot" day. We could sense it already when we woke up in the morning to the noise of explosions. On the main road, a whole Nazi armored division was passing by in battle order — I think it was the 26th — moving from our Adriatic sector to the one now more threatened — in the Rome and Anzio area. The ground was shaking under the noise of the tanks and the explosions. The British were attacking about three kilometers to the east of Navelli. The tanks proceeded slowly — jumping forward then stopping, all hermetically sealed up. The British fighter-bombers circled in the sky, then came down to attack and disrupt movement on the road.

The British air attack was in progress for three hours — always about three kilometers from Navelli. The fourth hour passed in a similar manner. I was in the square of Navelli. Everybody in the village was taking shelter, fearing the attack would reach the village as well. I observed how the German soldiers, the moment they reached the sheltered area of Navelli, opened the hatches of their armored vehicles and began to laugh. Well, for them it must be nothing new.

The armored cars were all dirty, filled with smoke and vibrating with their engines operating. One Panzer crossed the square with a German soldier sitting on the open turret. His face was grimaced with pain, both his legs shattered by British fire. In the square they took him down and carried him away.

Towards noon the British halted their attacks. In four hours they had managed to hit six tanks, which were now disabled in the square. Their crews covered them with branches and straw bales.

At about 1 p.m., Allied aircraft attacked the village. Their target: the tanks concentrated around our house, on the road and the yards. I managed to see two huge fire flashes about 30 meters away, even before I heard the explosions. I was quick enough to duck amidst the piercing noise of splinters flying everywhere, as the house shook in all directions; then I turned and saw Father with his fingers in his ears, his mouth open and his face grimaced, as he ducked under the arch of the doorway as the entire house seemed to crumble around us. The explosions created shock waves that stung my ears. Despite all the bombs, not a single tank was hit in a 30-meter radius of the house. In a moment of calm, we rushed out of the house and met Renato Osmo-Morris, who greeted us poker-faced — "What, you're still alive?" For the rest of the day I felt terribly lethargic. Doctor Osmo-Morris and some members of the "gang" who have had battle experience told me that this was "battle shock" as a consequence of the four hours of aerial attack, and then the direct hit.

26 JANUARY 1944

This evening we attacked! I was allowed to participate, too.

The objective was a German ammunitions dump near the road fork, mostly containing artillery shells that we needed. It was guarded by military police. At about 8.30 p.m. we moved out, armed only with some pistols and hand grenades. The order was to act as quickly and silently as possible. It was a very clear night. While the rest skirted the position through the fields I decided to go straight down the road. I ran quickly and the Germans didn't notice me.

It was very strange but I didn't feel any emotion. My head felt empty, focused solely on the ammunitions dump.

97

After about 100 meters, I reached the site. I threw myself into the ditch and started checking the boxes and shells. Then, weighted down and bent over by some 40 kilos of shells, I ran across the field as quick as possible, to where the rest of the group was waiting. I showed them how to use the handle of the boxes, and together with Luigi Alterio I returned again, this time through the fields. We sensed some movement from the Nazis' direction. A convoy was moving along the road. We pressed ourselves to the ground. Then, when the headlights shone in the direction of the sentry, we proceeded leapfrog fashion. After five minutes, we were back again. Then the other six started out, two by two. Everything proceeded well — swiftly and without any surprises. Even George got his first taste of action there. The Nazis didn't notice a thing, and we started back, loaded like mules with ammunition. After half an hour on a very uneven road, we reached the cave where we deposited our booty. I had half dislocated my shoulder with the load. We were all very pleased, and Aurelio congratulated me for the "cool" I had demonstrated at the age of just 16. I was very pleased, but only now have begun to feel the emotional impact of what I did. I returned home very tired, telling everyone we had trouble with the radio and couldn't hear any news.

A lot of Germans are passing through. A typical episode is the incident of the motorcyclist who by chance told us his real identity: he was of Polish origin, drafted into the army against his will. He was very angry — swearing — and told us that he had freed a whole truckload of British POWs. In his opinion, the German front line was like a piece of glass that the Allies could break through with one good punch, as everybody was so fed up.

For one day, a platoon of paratroopers — mostly 17- to 18-year-old boys– settled down in Navelli for a short rest from the front line. Two of them sat in our kitchen. One said that next April the Germans would land in England, while the second boy called him an idiot. He must be about 17, from Ulm, and complained, "When we were at school we were always told about our victories. Then later we were sent to the war and saw only defeats. When we were in Russia and asked where the Luftwaffe was they told us 'in Italy.' Here we asked the same question and the answer was they're in France. And there we are told that the Luftwaffe was in Germany. But the fact is — we don't see any German aircraft."

The first boy told us that his friend was under suspicion because he had allegedly already defected to the British, and when a group of British soldiers had been taken prisoner, he was found among them. Another soldier came in and called them to move out. They saluted him with the words, "*Heil Sieg und nie mehr Krieg!*" (Hail victory and no more war!) In the evening they left Navelli, after plundering a few houses and stealing some ham and bicycles from the farmers.

Our economic situation is getting worse. We eat badly and very little. Father gets more and more worried. We don't know where to escape to. All the time we hope the fascists will "forget us" for some reason. That's what Degen and Billig like to believe. Mother will have to go to Aquila again.

February 1944

Mother returned from Aquila shaken and frightened: the word being passed around is to flee and hide. She was upset following a very dangerous encounter in the middle of a street in Aquila. She and Mrs. Degen were having a conversation with another Jewish woman, when two Republican fascists appeared. They were combing the area for any Jew they could find. They arrested the woman on the spot. One of them — a man of the *Questura* — asked the second one, pointing his finger at Mother and Mrs. Degen, "What about them?" The second policeman answered, "No, let them go." Mother found shelter for the night in a monastery, and the next morning returned home as quickly as possible. This has put all of us on edge.

Almost every day, a score of Flying Fortresses flies over our heads. They perform a very tight turn, and test their weapons. The lead plane shoots a red or white signal rocket and then they release their bombs on Popoli, which is now a very strategic road fork with an important bridge across the Aterno-Pescara River.

The weather now is somewhat better. We walk about on the higher road in Navelli with George and the "gang" and, in the evenings, as has been the case for the last five months, we meet to listen to the radio. For the last five months we have gotten only disappointments. Even on the Anzio front the Allies are stranded, contained in a very small bridgehead and unable to advance.

8 FEBRUARY 1944

Father and Livio went up the mountain to gather pinecones for our fireplace. They returned in the afternoon, and I went out for my daily visit to George. I am quite busy there. I am now reproducing topographic maps of the Navelli area and to the south, all the way to the Majella. It is quite difficult and methodic work. I was just crossing the square where for the last few days a unit of cavalierly and horse-drawn supplies commanded by a Captain Müller (F.P.N. W-44669) has been camped, when a convoy of trucks with four-barreled anti-aircraft guns stopped in the village. Five minutes later, 11 British fighter-bombers appeared. I took shelter behind the door of the Osmo-Morris' house. The British detected the trucks. They came in low, dropping bombs and strafing the ground. I would like to have seen this show clearly, but each time I put out my head, I had to jump back and hide behind the door. The noise was tremendous: explosions and heavy machine-gun fire. All hell broke loose. About four meters away from where I was crouching, a small German gun unleashed a round of fire. The crew stayed solid as stones — they seemed to be extensions of the gun, completely unafraid of the enemy's fire. One of the low-flying fighters was encircled in a ball of fire and began to climb for altitude as it burned. From the Germans came a shout of "Hurrah!" I couldn't see where the aircraft crashed. The remaining planes tried to attack — low again — but were unable to cope with the heavy ground fire, and with that one loss they escaped to the south.

The airplane — a Spitfire — crashed behind Navelli on the other slope of the hill. I arrived there within ten minutes, together with a group of Germans and local Italians. The plane was all broken up and smashed, and near the wreckage of the airplane was the body of the pilot, broken too. He lay half-burned in a pool of blood that had colored the snow crimson. He was lying on his back, his hands palms up, his stomach and his left thigh torn open in a mess of bloody flesh. The pilot's left foot had been severed in his boot and thrown some 10 meters away with what remained of his leg. His face was horrible — like a mask — empty without the skull, one eye hanging down. A few yellowish hairs were stuck to his forehead. He wore the rank of captain, and it seemed that he had died the moment he was hit. Pierino, seeing all this and smelling the stench of burned human flesh, threw up and left. The German soldiers abused the dead body. Some of them were drunk and kicked the corpse. The Italians were offended by this behavior and a row developed in the light of the still burning parts of the airplane. Evening came, and the body of the dead pilot was left there alone.

The whole village was thrown into turmoil. German soldiers went around shooting in the air and calling for the village to be burned down in reprisal for the clash with the Italians near the downed plane, as well as the beating they received. They arrested the mayor and literally threw him through our door towards Father, demanding he translate what he had to say. The poor man was completely terrorized, as were the farmers. Indeed, it seemed like the end of the world. Everywhere one could hear shooting, drunken German soldiers calling for revenge — breaking into some houses and threatening to burn down the whole village. Nevertheless, we went to listen to the radio. To avoid slipping, George lit a candle. At once, they started shooting at us. We extinguished the candle and crawled on the ground until we reached George's house in the pitch dark, followed by shots.

When I returned home, I heard that Emil had paid a visit. How come? L.21063 was passing through Navelli, on its way to Cassino, and Emil had not forgotten us. He stopped the car and left with us no less than six loaves of bread! But he had to continue at once. At home I found, among the whole confusion, an elderly German soldier, a painter. He spoke sadly about his comrades and what they were doing outside. He told us about his service in Serbia and how Yugoslav partisans had killed Germans in the streets of Belgrade. He added that he should not speak of such things, but those Slavs "were fighting for their country." Strange that he should have noticed it only now. And he should not have talked about it at all, but he spoke anyway.

The night passed with shots and shouts. George discovered that the Germans had taken all the documents from the dead pilot. He found only a copper coin, which he kept as a souvenir. We wrote down the serial number of the airplane.

The next morning, a commission of enquiry arrived from Aquila with two S.S. officers. The secretary of the council invited my father to help translate. Those two officers were very "correct" — asking if everybody present was a fascist. Of course everybody was — my father, too... Employing

103

some diplomacy, Father tried to turn the whole episode around, seeing that the two S.S. were reasonable people. After a long discussion, they all reached the conclusion that the drunken soldiers were guilty, but asked to have two or three Italians held as hostages with the promise of releasing them the very next day. The three Italians, identified by the soldiers as the people who started the row, were taken away. The whole village was relieved. The three hostages returned later that very evening.

When it was dark, George, Ugo and Aurelio paid their last respects to the dead pilot and put him in a coffin, two days after the battle. The Germans took him away.

At George's home we had an important visitor: the chief of a partisan unit and his second in command. He is an Italian army lieutenant called Ubaldo. For good reason, he did not tell us his family name. He lives in the next valley. But now, during the winter, they do only propaganda work and assist escaped British POWs in the area. I was introduced, as well. They decided that Iginio Quintilio and I would serve as "dispatch riders" between the two groups. Lieutenant Ubaldo had heard about the shells and explosives we had captured and was convinced that something useful could be made of them. He would look for some solution for the Mitra magazines. He left at night.

10 FEBRUARY 1944

Father was called to the town hall: Captain Ehrig, his driver and batman Berger were passing through Navelli, and wanted to greet him. Berger told Father a very moving story, while Captain Ehrig smoked and listened, saying nothing. Berger said that he was a pianist from Berlin, and had had a Jewish friend in Berlin, "like you, Mr. Fleischmann." A few weeks earlier, while driving the car with Ehrig, he had gotten a flat tire. Suddenly he felt somebody embracing him and calling him by his name. He was surprised to see his Jewish colleague from Berlin. Berger told us how tears had come from his eyes: here was a Jew, persecuted and banished but still embracing his former friend in Nazi uniform with no rebuke at all. Berger asked, "What is the sense of all this persecution and death? Why? The Jews are people like everybody else." Ehrig listened in silence. He couldn't add anything there for he is a captain, but his silence was a form of agreement. Then the two Germans proceeded on their way. Father returned home, very moved.

No more lessons with Giosi. Mr. Giosi left Navelli together with Advocate Santucci, and went to stay in a village in the middle of the mountains — Bominaco — far away from the Germans and the bombings. We remain here at the mercy of fate.

For over a month now, there has been a soldier from the Hermann Göring Division — perhaps half a deserter — here in Navelli. He left an amphibious vehicle in the sports gymnasium, the former site of the bakery ovens. A few days ago, he sold the farmers the tires off its wheels, as well as blankets and gas masks. He lives in a room formerly used by the Nazis and passes his day in the house of...the Jew, Degen. Quite a deserter...

105

The old husband of Michelina, Nicolantonio, was caught by the German sentries one night, stealing from the amphibious car. He was thoroughly beaten up, and in the morning some farmers brought him home, wounded.

Life goes on — hunting for food with a Damocles sword hanging over our heads. In the morning we are not sure what will happen in the afternoon, and we go to bed with the terror of being woken up by fascists at the door. In the morning, we rise with the fear that we may not see noon. The news we hear on the radio is quite disappointing. If it weren't for the big victories of the Red Army, I do not know where our morale would be.

24 FEBRUARY 1944

Mr. Billig had a *Yahrzeit*[15] to observe, and he came to our house with Degen in the morning to pray. During the middle of the service, Mrs. Billig arrived, very pale. Leaning on the door, she whispered: "The fascists are here with a truck to take us away." Everybody was panic-stricken! Billig and Degen ran off in terror. Father and Mother seemed to have lost their heads. I tried to convince them to come with me, but they didn't want to listen, so I left, alone.

---

15 The anniversary of a relative's death, marked by reciting the *Kaddish* (mourner's prayer), lighting a candle, and other acts of commemoration for the deceased.

Within a few minutes, I was at George's. He was in the middle of shaving, and was greatly agitated. I asked him what could be done. "Escape," he replied. While he was dressing, his mother arrived and told us that this time the fascists were after them, too. But they were quite calm. They are British citizens, they reasoned, so nothing would ever happen to them. But George did not accept that. Quickly, we burned the topographic maps, and dashed into the street to look for Aurelio, who followed us. At the edge of Navelli in "Siberia," we took leave from George, who had an address where he could find refuge. He headed up the mountain road. Aurelio told me to hurry up to the "high square" in Navelli, where he and three other partisans would wait for me and take me to a safe place.

I left alone, feeling the whole world spinning around me. I could see Father, Mother and Livio down in the village, walking across the square, escorted by the local guard. I didn't know where he was taking them.

The local people looked depressed but they didn't dare express what they thought because of the fascists. I managed not to be seen by my family, and reached the upper square. Aurelio, Ugo and two other people from the group were already waiting for me. Tensely, we started to move out towards the upper exit from Navelli leading to the mountain. But we had hardly taken a few steps when we found ourselves face to face with a Republican fascist with a paper in his hand. He asked me if I was Luigi Fleischmann. "Yes, that's me," I admitted. "Well, in five minutes you have to present yourself at the town hall," he said, and went on his way. He couldn't have been more foolish!

We moved out, crossing some fields, and started to climb up the mountain, in the direction of Civitaretenga. I walked with a very heavy heart, having chosen to disregard what was happening to my family.

After reaching Civitaretenga — which was really a very small place — I was taken to a big, old house where a half-crazy painter who belonged to the "movement" lived. An hour later, George was there, too. It had taken him so long to reach the place because he had chosen a roundabout route.

Our spirits were very low. The hours passed and we had nothing to eat. Who knew what was going on in Navelli? George bet (he is always betting) that nobody would be deported. Anyway, we decided that if we found ourselves alone, we would start marching south to the Majella, and try to cross the line. I was really lucky to have new boots.

The half-crazy painter showed us a hiding place in case they searched the place. It was in a walled cupboard with some 100 books — you took out two shelves of books, the wall moved and behind it was a small room, large enough for two people to live in.

Time passed very slowly. In the evening, at last, they brought us something to eat. A partisan brought some four or five kilos of roast beef. We ate the rare treat, but under the circumstances couldn't really enjoy the taste. At about midnight we went to sleep, while high up in the sky a lonely British reconnaissance plane threw flares. What had happened in Navelli?

25 FEBRUARY 1944

We woke up in the morning, very tense, and waited for Aurelio. At about 11 a.m. he finally arrived with Ugo, and we heard the story.

Everything had gone well. They had already prepared weapons to attack the fascists and free the deported people. But in the end it was not necessary. Here is the story, as it unfolded.

A few minutes after my escape, Mario De Nardis arrived at our house. Leaving the fascist guards outside, he entered alone and told my parents to run away. Then he left. Escorted by the local guard Italo Petracchini, my family first went to George's house, but hearing that the British nationals were wanted too, the guard took them all to his own house, where they were still hiding. I felt so relieved. George after all, had "won his bet." Billig had found a hiding place in the bakery oven — which fortunately had been turned off the day before. Degen welcomed the fascists with a few sacks of flour. They took away the flour and left the Jews. But the most amusing story is what happened to the British family. It is now almost two months since they moved to the upper part of Navelli, and their new domicile has two doors. One of the fascists positioned himself at the main entrance, while the Osmo-Morris's were getting ready with their luggage…and they had a lot of luggage. Then they decided to escape and leave by the second door, leaving all their possessions behind. But doctor Osmo-Morris felt that he had to be honest. So he went to the fascist guarding the front door, hugged him and told him: "Look here, we're leaving by the back door, so please don't look in that direction," and forcibly stuffed some money into the man's pocket. Then, calmly, they left the house. Thus, nobody was apprehended.

The man in charge of this whole search operation was *Commissario*[16] Mario De Nardis. While his men were searching, he was at the town hall telling the secretary, the town mayor and the *maresciallo*[17] of the police that they must help to find the people he was looking for in every way possible. Then he went down to the square, called in his men, and started shouting at them about how useless they were in front of the whole village — who understood what was happening and were grinning at the "show." The *Commissario* shouted at the *Carabinieri* officer, ordering him to deliver the people he wanted — should he find them — into the hands of the German MPs as swiftly as possible, and then left, telling his men not to take all the luggage belonging to the missing persons they had come to take into custody, because "there was not enough room on the truck!"

Aurelio advised us not to move yet. Others might come back to search again, and anyway everybody was still hiding. They took advantage of the events to converse with a partisan who had come down from the mountain and tried to find a way to make contact with one of the British paratroopers. There was a lot of talk about them among the partisans. We stayed overnight in Civitaretenga.

16 Commissioner.
17 Marshal.

26 FEBRUARY 1944

In the evening, I returned with George to Navelli. At home, we welcomed each other joyfully. My family said jokingly that I was some good son... leaving them in the moment of danger and running away alone. I answered that I had told them to come with me at once. In the evening, while listening to the radio, we spoke of the dangerous situation we had just been through, and felt good about the outcome.

The *maresciallo* of the *Carabinieri* told my father that we must get away from Navelli and find some other place of shelter. He told us that De Nardis was detained for a whole day in Aquila by the S.S., until the Nazis received confirmation that no one was actually hiding in Navelli. (Who gave them this confirmation?) At least we should look for a different house to live in, they advised.

At home, of course, we were far from complacent. We had escaped once and were lucky. While the entire event had almost turned into a farce, the next time it could end very differently.

I was called to the command office of the German military police. Nothing very important. The man in charge, a *Feldwebel* with a wooden head who doesn't understand a thing and speaks only after asking somebody else's opinion, wanted to know how many radio sets there were in the village. He had received an order to register and then confiscate them all. But, he added, he "knows there are no radio sets left in the village." He really didn't care that everybody could listen to whatever news they chose. He simply didn't care.

111

And really, the only news that makes us happy is about the Eastern Front. The Soviets are advancing everywhere — in Poland, in Estonia. The Allied attack on Cassino failed. And here? Nothing moves.

Aurelio gave me two Italian newspapers he had acquired secretly from the south — across the front line. The two newspapers were December issues of the *Gazzetta del Mezzogiorno* from Bari. The news of course, was not news anymore, and therefore not of interest per se, but I was very curious to see papers from liberated areas. I showed them around at home and then gave them back to Aurelio.

Here, the British have scattered thousands of leaflets in German from airplanes or small balloons, for the German soldiers. The heading reads: *Das fünfte Jahr* — the fifth year. It carries news about the war, urging the Germans to surrender before things become even worse.

While descending the steps from George' house, I met his brother Renato Osmo-Morris, who told me that the Santucci mansion is now empty because Advocate Santucci had left for a more isolated and tranquil place — Bominaco. He wanted somebody to move in and keep an eye on the place. This could be a good chance to change our place of residence.

28 FEBRUARY 1944

We have moved. Mother and Livio sorted out two rooms of the mansion. That was quite a task because everything

112

was horribly broken, dirty and looted by the German troops who had passed through, and most of the house is unfit to live in. In the evening, we moved in. The weather has changed to snow again after January's snow almost melted away. It is snowing heavily.

We hope that in our new abode we will be able to enjoy some tranquility. The only inconvenience is that a half-witted priest, Don Beppe — called "Don Teppi" by Livio — lives in a room near ours. He is a silly priest, going around only in his cassock without trousers and torn socks to keep warm. He almost burned down a wing of the house using part of the furniture for firewood. It is unbelievable how this half-excommunicated priest talks. He badmouths his own religion, telling us, "It's all business," and that he holds services only because he gets money out of it while personally he doesn't believe in it. He believes only in business. He is a very unnerving neighbor, but we can't get rid of him.

Two people from Navelli have lent us a pile of blankets without even knowing us personally, because our old landlady couldn't give us her blankets.

March 1944

It is now March and our situation is getting worse day by day. George and his brother went to look for another place of shelter beyond Navelli. They reached a small village about 12 kilometers to the north, called Opi, lost in the

113

midst of the mountains. George returned completely ill after marching in the snow and mud, and now has a very bad fever.

We woke up in the middle of the night to loud knocks on the door and shouts of "*Aufmachen!*" (Open up!) We were quite scared. Father went to open the door and, to his horror, found himself facing the German MPs and some S.S. men. But they were not looking for us. They were after that German deserter from the "Hermann Göring" Division who was hiding in some wing of this mansion. After a few minutes they found him and took him away.

On the main road there is the usual traffic, but only by night. They don't dare travel in daylight, and almost every day Popoli gets its "quota" of bombs, shaking the surrounding mountains. Nothing new on the radio broadcast. The weather is still bad and dark, but the snow on the ground is melting. It's very wet snow.

5 March 1944

The Osmo-Morris family has left Navelli. Only George is left. He is very ill and Adriana remains with him. We still meet in his house, but the whole group is very depressed. Aurelio has decided not to take any new action in the near future. The only thing he did was throw away the road sign that read in German, "Beware — Area of Guerrilla Activity." But he did it mostly out of rage.

Lieutenant Ubaldo asked us to send the shells and

explosives in our possession to him at his headquarters in Caporciano. (There are Germans there, too.) He is sure he will be able to do something with them. At his request, we sent him the only "Mitra" magazine we have.

6 MARCH 1944

The Billig family left today, despite the weather. Their sense of fear was stronger than any bad weather. We believe they are going to Carapelle, quite far away and "lost" in the middle of the mountains. We were all very sad and dispirited. Father was in a very bad mood. We would like to leave, too.

Father decided to go to Bominaco to look for a possible hiding place. He took Livio with him. He was back in the evening brought by a car of one of the local landlords. He told us that Giosi — now also a refugee — happily welcomed him. Santucci, too. They told him to move to Bominaco and that we would all manage together somehow. Trying to be helpful, Giosi told Father that he would be ready to start learning German again, when he comes.

A few days ago, the police officer warned us that the Nazis have decided to search for us again — this time with German units. They are sure to be very different from the Italian fascists. He begged us to escape, and then departed.

At the town hall, the communal secretary De Guido

gave Father a new identity card as well as an empty one that we could fill in with whatever details we wanted. He even put an official stamp on it and wished Father all the best.

This evening, for the last time, I went to Quintilo's house to listen to the news on the radio. Aurelio heard there would be a great German search action in the coming days. He has decided to withdraw to the mountains with the entire "group," armed, taking the escaped Russian POW with them, as well. There they will join up with Lieutenant Ubaldo's group and hole up in the mountains between Navelli and Caporciano, taking only a defensive stance should enemy search parties attack them. I was really sorry not to be able to join them this time, but tomorrow morning we leave Navelli and nobody must see us — especially not the military police — because nobody is allowed to leave the village. The radio told us the same news, commentaries from Candidus[18] and Soviet victories which can't help us at all here in Italy. Be what may, I took leave from everybody. We were very moved by the farewells, but Aurelio and Ugo promised they would come visit me, if and when it was at all possible. Bominaco is no more than a hamlet in the mountains that must have 200 inhabitants at best!

Some farmers gave me a gift — a basket full of bread, fat and other foodstuffs to take with us — and I was very moved. As I left, they wished us well, saying, "May God bless you!"

18 A famous radio commentator.

116

7 March 1944

It was freezing in the morning. The ground was hard and frozen, but the sky was clearing. It was not even 7 a.m. and we were already on the move. The horse-drawn carriage with our luggage and a few other things had already left. We gave Adriana the firewood that was left and then we departed — under the curious and surprised eyes of the foolish priest Don Beppe. We managed to leave Navelli without being seen. We quickly reached the main road, and began our trek to Bominaco with the frost biting at our limbs. Under my arm I carried a loaf of bread covered with paper. As we left Navelli behind us, Father commented bitterly, "Here you have it — the Wandering Jews."

We walked for almost an hour without seeing a soul in the fields. It was too cold. An intermittent rumbling followed us. Who knows why the front line woke up today in particular? We were already in the next plain, not far from Caporciano, walking on a terribly muddy back road between the fields. We still had to go up that mountain to that far-away castle, behind which lay Bominaco.

While crossing a muddy field road, an armed German soldier with a steel helmet on a motorcycle came our way. He looked at us but made no comment, and went on patrolling the back road. What was he doing there?

We reached Caporciano. The town was totally silent and dead. At 9 in the morning, all this looked very strange. The sun was out. It was a nice day, but very cold. The horse-drawn wagon with our belongings took a longer but smoother route. As we climbed up a narrow street

117

between the houses, we suddenly saw armed German and fascist soldiers coming down from the top! We quickly took cover and let them pass. We looked down towards the lower part of the village and were horrified to see the whole town surrounded, with Nazi-fascists searching the place. Then we understood why that soldier was patrolling the muddy fields. We were in a very dangerous predicament. If we had been caught, it would have been the end for us. We walked on. Terrified farmers gazed at us from their houses, but we pushed on, and after fifteen minutes of narrow lanes, backyards and small fields and vineyards, we managed to leave the village without falling into the dragnet of the Nazi search parties. We reached the road to Bominaco. We had something to eat, and were able to see from our vantage point above Caporciano how the carriage with our belongings had been stopped in the square by the Germans, but released after a short exchange of words.

We are now in Bominaco — about eight kilometers northwest of Navelli. This small hamlet is "boxed" into a closed valley, dominated by the ruins of a castle. Bominaco is hidden from the main highway. We are high up, at an altitude of almost 900 meters, 200 meters higher than Navelli. Only one road leads to Bominaco.

Giosi and Santucci awaited us, together with other people like the Aloisio brothers, who, it seems, do not know our true identity. We received two small cellar-like rooms in the house of a professor Servetto, a landlord of Bominaco. Our hearts sank when we beheld those two little rooms with a low ceiling and two very small windows facing the road. But Giosi tried to cheer us up, and asked when Father would be ready to resume his lessons. For hours, the windows rattled from the faraway gunfire. Up here in Bominaco, we hear it much more clearly than in Navelli.

The farmers of this little village sought to help us at once. Somebody brought a chair, somebody else, a water container. These gestures of kindness were very moving.

Livio and I settled down in the kitchen — one of the rooms with a fireplace. I found a place for myself on a bed frame with a door for a mattress. Livio rested on something similar. In the other room, Mother and Father lay down on a few empty flour sacks next to a smoky oil lamp, the luggage spread about around them. A true abode for fugitives. Very arduous conditions.

The next morning I climbed with Livio up to the castle on the hill. We had a breath-taking view. Clouds and fog were spread out under us, and we could see both plains — the plain of Navelli, and then the "bottleneck" of Civitaretenga to our left. Down to our right sat Bominaco, then the plain of Caporciano, and to the south rising high above it all — the Majella, all white and blue. To the east was the Gran Sasso and to the west, Mount Sirente — a big mountain I had never seen before from Navelli.

Somehow we settled into our new lodgings. So as not to be occupied all the time thinking about our present state and the uncertainty of the future, Father will start giving German lessons to Giosi again in a couple of days. In order to help us, Santucci asked Father if he could teach English to Professor Servetto's two daughters, who were born in

Chile, as well as to the son of a local landlord, Michele Agrippa, and his mother Mrs. Agrippa, who is a teacher in the village. Two Italian officers from Sicily are hiding in the hamlet, as well. In the coming days they will try to cross the fighting line.

We have been here for a couple of days already and the front is still rumbling. It's a continuous noise, impossible to distinguish one from the next. The windows, houses and ground shake all the time — like an earthquake. But the farmers take absolutely no heed.

I was sitting up near the castle in the midst of a foggy rain thinking about my situation and looking a little nostalgically in the direction of Navelli when I heard somebody down below in Bominaco calling my name. Maybe two or three voices. I ran down the hill and found Ugo, Giuseppino, Pierino and Aurelio. They were dirty and muddy. They had come down from their mountain encampment to visit me and see how I was doing. I was really moved.

They are camped near Mount S. Erasmo amidst the snow, mud and rain. So far, the Germans have not searched for them. And if things go on like this, the two groups will secretly return to their villages.

Ugo recalled that a girl he went to school with lives here in Bominaco with her family. They live in a house near ours. There were many people there, and Ugo introduced me to everyone. They knew about our arrival and wanted to get acquainted with my family. The two brothers — the officers in hiding who helped us when we arrived — Mario and Gaetano, belong to this family, the Aloisios. There is the old father, Giovanni, the mother, and two daughters, Anna and Elena — very nice people. They wanted me to visit them in the evenings. They had noticed that in the last few days I seemed quite bored, and offered for me to listen to the news on their radio.

After an hour, my friends left and went back to the mountains. Now, once again, I had a place to get news. In the evening, I went to the Aloisios'. Father and Mother went too, and in a short time they got well acquainted. They are really very noble and warm people, and the friendship they exhibit is very moving. They too subsist with great difficulties, but at least they are lucky not to be persecuted Jews. I also met an Italian soldier at their home — a refugee named Francesco Spada from S. Severo. We have become good friends.

I wonder what poor George is doing — left alone in Navelli and very ill?

Within a few days, the German search action in Caporciano was over. But, strangely enough, nobody so much as came up to Bominaco. Only yesterday evening, a lone German car came to the hamlet. I don't know why, of course, but it left after half an hour.

I went down to Caporciano to make contact with the second-in-command of the partisan unit in this area. I had already met him at George's house in Navelli; his name is Antonio Conte. He told me that I am now, automatically, attached to his "gang" — with the same job of "errand boy" as I had in Navelli, but that in the upcoming days I should present myself personally to Lieutenant Ubaldo — who is called the *Perugino*. Antonio Conte told me that during

121

the German search operation, some men of his "attack" group entered the village and set the registry office of the local town hall on fire, destroying all of the lists of the inhabitants, the names of people in the army call-ups and so forth, so they would not fall into the hands of the Germans.

The Degen family is hiding in Caporciano, but we don't visit them at all because we don't want to be seen together. It is better to stay completely apart.

10 March 1944

In the afternoon, the weather subsided and I decided, without saying anything to the family, to make a trip to Navelli. After all, eight kilometers is not a big deal and I managed to take Francesco with me. In Caporciano, I entered the house where Lieutenant Ubaldo had found shelter. (I left Francesco outside.) I reported to him and he confirmed that from now on I belong to his group — the 2nd company of the "Gran Sasso" brigade. I told him I was on my way to Navelli to find out how George was and he asked me to see if there was a way to bring him out of Navelli.

After walking for more than an hour and a half, partly through mud, and crossing two hills to enter Navelli unseen, I arrived in the village. Very moved, I ran down the steps, trying not to be seen, and at last entered the room where George was laying with a very high fever.

Adriana was very worried about him. She was afraid that the Germans might find out that one of the Englishmen was still hiding in Navelli. Then I went to see the Quintilio family. They welcomed me with joy. When I left them after a short visit, they gave me some fresh eggs to take home with me, but I left them with George. He needed them more than I. He was too weak even to greet me.

The road back seemed endless. We had to cross the whole muddy plain and that slowed us down. Because of the darkness and the mud, I stumbled on some rusty barbed wire and got slightly gashed. To avoid an infection Francesco burned my skin and the wound with a whole box of matches. When we reached Caporciano, we woke up the pharmacist and he treated the wound. Francesco and I arrived back in Bominaco under cover of darkness. My family, whom I had not told about my intended trip back to Navelli, were already worrying about me.

We understand from the radio that the last battle of Cassino has ended in another failure. It truly looks as though the Allies won't move until spring. I never thought last September that I would be speaking the truth when I made that prognosis. I only meant it in jest...

In the evening, while my family was talking with the Aloisios and listening to the radio, Mario, one of the sons, recalled how, when he was serving in Croatia, the Italian army did whatever possible to save the Jews from the Germans. The elderly Mr. Aloisio talked about the equality of all human beings, and could not understand the reason for all this hate and persecution against a different faith or race. Father understood that they have grasped we are Jews and, after hearing this kind of talk over a number of evenings, said so outright.

Our life in Bominaco is quite tough. There isn't enough food or money to eat in a normal way. We've gotten used to eating bread with bran, black bread — and only two slices a day. In the morning, when we wake up, we receive two slices of thin black bread. Father gives us these two slices with a particular expression on his face. We even count the crumbs. For lunch we sometimes have a *polenta*[19] of maize flour, but mostly we eat lentils and chickpeas as we did in Navelli…but in smaller quantities: a chick pea soup and a plate of lentils, cooked and warmed in water. But our spirits are more or less high. We keep our good humor and take things philosophically, imagining that the food we eat is good. Nevertheless, Father is skinny; we all are skinny, for that matter. My clothes are falling apart and the only good things I am wearing are my boots.

Mother walks every evening to the fountain to bring home water. The farmers here are wonderful. Nobody says anything but they start bringing us cheese, bread and eggs, and give us these presents with an embarrassed expression written on their faces — as if they were ashamed for having to do this. A priest lives in this small village. They warned me about this man in Caporciano, since it is rumored he is a spy for the Germans and that he has already betrayed two English escaped prisoners. But on Sunday, in his sermon in the church, he told the farmers that there are persecuted people who have found shelter in the village

19 A dish made from boiled cornmeal.

who are in need of help and, without naming anybody, he called on them to assist us. We felt quite embarrassed to receive help from these poor farmers who fight so hard to get something out of their unrewarding soil.

I went to Opi to tell the doctor's family of George's situation. I had to follow a very narrow path for over three kilometers amidst a small, long and narrow valley that opens up into Opi — a hamlet of about 160-170 people, above the next valley of the river Aterno. From Opi, when the weather is clear, one can get a good view up the plain of S. Gregorio and, even further away, veiled by fog, the houses of Aquila. We decided to return to Navelli with Doctor Osmo-Morris to take George away. He will stay at our house in Bominaco until he is well again.

16 MARCH 1944

After two days in Navelli, Doctor Osmo-Morris and I carried George and Adriana to Bominaco in a carriage. George looked like a skeleton, thin and worn out. The illness had really "done him in." We put him in a little room above our two rooms. And so we have somebody to share our chickpeas and lentils with, to sit with us near the half-lit fireplace in the dark and cold evenings to the weak light of the oil lamp — and he still is able to laugh at the jokes we tell to pass the time.

Indeed, had we not maintained our good spirits during those long dark winter days, with all the dangers, I think we would have hanged ourselves. Anyway, we always find something to joke about, some funny word, something to laugh at. Now, for instance, we make fun of the chickpeas and lentils "dressed" in hot water, which George and Adriana have to eat with us.

Father is giving his lessons again in the house above us where the Servetto family lives. They are very nice people. He is also giving lessons to the Advocate Santucci and his family.

During the day I walk around with George, whose health is slowly improving. We stroll about the village, and up to the square where there are two beautiful churches — one very ancient from Roman times, the other from the Middle Ages. They are very romantic and beautiful — really works of art!

Among the farmers, who are all very helpful to us, is the wife of the local night watchman, the mail carrier, Doralice Andreucci. She is a very poor and simple woman who helps Mother in every possible way, fetching water, making bread, and bringing some vegetables, cheese or milk for us.

In the evenings at Aloisios' house, we listen to the news for a few hours. The radio reports are like pure oxygen for us.

It snowed again, but winter is on its way out. After the snow, it rained and the weather has turned mild.

I often go down to Caporciano to hear from Lieutenant Ubaldo if there is anything new. But the orders are always the same. Do nothing until the good weather arrives, and try to do some propaganda work in the meantime. Gather your strength for things to come. I met the second-in-command, Antonio Conte, a wild person but with a heart of gold. He told me that if my family needs anything, he could always find some way to help them. Ubaldo told me about the "Mitra" magazines. He had found a blacksmith in a nearby village, S. Pio, who was now trying to build some of them in his workshop. He still didn't know if the magazines would work well. He was building them of iron sheeting taken from some destroyed German trucks.

George is getting better every day. We pass pleasant hours together. From time to time, someone from his family comes from Opi to visit him. George thinks all the time about how to find a way to contact some of the British officers who are believed to be operating from the surrounding mountains. He questions the farmers who, rumor has it, often see somebody tall with blond hair and a rucksack on his back, crossing the woods in the hills. Ubaldo also insisted this was true, and George told him he would start searching as well, the moment he felt well enough.

The watch-woman called me. There were three British in her house, escaped POWs. They were eating when I walked in. I exchanged some words with them. They were terribly hungry. They wanted to try and cross the line, being fed up with walking around the mountains for the last seven months chased like wild wolves.

Mother made some "important" acquaintances while going to the well for water, some very kind women. The people of this small hamlet are very simple and primitive. They live a very hard life between the mountains and the stones in their little barren fields, working the whole day together with their donkeys like slaves. They may never get even the minimum they need to live out of these fields, but they remain good and kind human beings, the way only simple people can be. For instance, they refuse to be paid for the firewood they have brought us from the start. They bring us presents, including food. They have seen the black bread we bring to the baker's oven. They are very embarrassed to give us food — and we are embarrassed to have to need it. They tell us all the time that it is customary in their village to offer food to anybody coming to live with them. Of course, this is not true, but they say so in order to bring us gifts without it undermining our dignity.

I spend hours at the Aloisios. I like to talk about different things with Anna, one of the daughters, a very young schoolteacher who, in fact, has never taught in school. She talks like a convinced fascist — but only in ideological terms, for after all she sees the criminal nature of the party and its responsibility for the war. But she's a romantic and likes it that way. She likes to argue freely about anything. Their door is always open, and indeed I am at their house for hours, talking, reading or listening to the radio.

After about ten days with us, George Osmo-Morris felt relatively better and left for Opi and his family. I was to be the liaison between the British and Lieutenant Ubaldo in Caporciano. The same morning I left for Navelli, together with George's brother Renato, to look for food. As usual, I stopped by the partisan headquarters — a room squeezed between a pigpen and a chicken coop. In this small farmhouse there is always movement of messengers in and out, all dressed like farmers…or real farmers. I always go in when I have something to report in this somewhat dangerous work.

To enter Caporciano unseen, as I did then with Renato Osmo-Morris, or when I go alone, I always have to take a difficult shortcut where you could break a leg. You have to go unobserved because even here there are Nazi soldiers, though they belong to a small unit that the partisans never bother, and I believe they never will.

The house where Lieutenant Ubaldo lives is on the slope of the village between the mountain and the plain. Out of curiosity, I crossed the little square and saw the blackened walls of the town council house, gutted by the fire set by the partisans. The Germans didn't care about the fire so, as always, I reached headquarters, between the pigs and the chickens. Ubaldo told me that last night the shells and explosives had been brought from Navelli, and he already had an idea what to do with them. After an hour-and-a-half walk, we entered Navelli, taking all possible precautions. Renato remained in the old part of the town, while I went down to the Quintilos. In the evening, we all met there. Aurelio and Ugo told me to report to Ubaldo that in the days ahead they would visit him to talk about different plans of action. Aurelio was thinking about launching attacks on the steep turns of the road to Popoli, and wanted some help from the company.

Under the cover of darkness, Aurelio took Renato and me to the Russian's hiding place — the cellar of a half-destroyed house. His condition was quite appalling. Having had a few years of medical school, Renato stated that he had pneumonia. The Russian was smoking, and the whole cellar was full of smoke. We could barely stand the stench. The straw was wet, and cold air penetrated everywhere. The Russian was resting on the wet ground, smoking chestnut leaves instead of tobacco. He was too weak to talk, and only gazed at us with pitiful eyes. When he recognized me as the former interpreter, he smiled. Renato and Aurelio decided to evacuate him from Navelli to Opi, where his father the doctor could take care of him. But it was 13 kilometers away across the mountains, and for somebody in his state it could have been both difficult and very dangerous. But the Russian had expressed his wish to go, so we left him with the plan to take him with us the next morning, by donkey.

At 4 a.m., Renato and I were on the top of the hill behind Navelli. Snow had fallen during the night and a very cold wind was blowing, but the sky was already clear, with all the stars twinkling in the sky. To the south, there were sparks of light and rumbling sounds of the battlefront, but I didn't care any longer. The more I saw it, the angrier I got. For the last three months the British have been sitting there under our noses and don't even budge.

Aurelio arrived but told us that the Russian couldn't leave in such weather. He would be sent for in the next few days. I reported all this to Ubaldo and Antonio Conte in Caporciano. They assured me that if the Russian came to Opi, the partisans would do everything possible to alleviate the extra burden on the English family, including providing food for him.

One morning, after the weather cleared, Francesco Spada

called me to tell me there were two English POWs outside Bominaco. I went to see them: two young men, a Scotsman named Ben and the other a very young man, Leo — who had been taken prisoner on the Majella and later escaped by jumping off a train. I took them down near Caporciano with Francesco, and went to report to Ubaldo. Ubaldo gave me an address in the village of Filetto — the headquarters of the brigade, some 40 kilometers to the north; the Englishmen would have to report there. I returned to the hill, but they were gone. Francesco told me that the pair didn't trust me and thought I went to turn them over to the Germans, so they had run in the direction of Opi. I ran after them, but I didn't see anyone so I returned.

Lieutenant Ubaldo told me that last night, part of his company attacked a Nazi convoy and succeeded in seizing explosives. He told me many things about what is going on. For instance, a few days ago he arranged a meeting near S. Severo-Erasmo in the middle of the mountains with someone reputed to be the commander of a group from the Fontecchio valley. It was raining hard, and Ubaldo was suspicious, fearing it might be a trap. So he went accompanied by Antonio Conte and another three men, all armed with sub-machine guns. The trio remained hidden. When the man he was to meet appeared, Ubaldo went out in the open and gave him his hand. This was the signal for the four armed men to surround the stranger with their weapons and force him to identify himself. But he really was the commander of the group, and had come alone and unarmed. Ubaldo smiled and added that in this kind of underground war, you can never be too cautious. He is right. He has never disclosed his family name, and even his second-in-command, Antonio, ignores this fact. With the other chiefs he is only known as the *Perugino*, although he is from Gubbio. Politically, he is not a communist. On the contrary: in meetings he is always arguing with Bruno, the communist from Navelli.

One morning in the last days of March, two young men from Navelli cheerfully arrived with the Russian astride a donkey, but he was still very ill. One could see it on his face. Quickly I showed them the road to Opi. There he would be taken care of.

The next day I went to Opi. The narrow three-kilometer-long valley I have to walk through to get there is now changing beautifully. The winter at last is over, and one can see farmers grazing sheep and working their fields. Arriving in Opi, I went straight to George's room. He lives separately from his family. There I ran into the two Englishmen who had run away. They rose to greet me, somewhat embarrassed, and said they were sorry for not trusting me. George was surprised that I already knew them, and when I told him the story, we all laughed. The Russian is getting better, and soon will be back to full health. The doctor was amazed by the constitution of the man. He believed that anybody else would already have been dead; the Russian had an extraordinarily strong body. He was lying on some empty sacks in a small room near George, and was very happy when I visited him. He knows only a few words of Italian. His name is Afanacio Meseyvitch, a Ukrainian. He's not very young. In fact he's over 40.

It is always the same sad state of affairs in Bominaco. For me, it is really a relief to walk around the mountains among the partisans and the British former POWs — to see the open sky and nature's rebirth now, with the arrival of spring. At least there I eat more than at home. Father teaches to an "audience" that really learns, and that makes him happy. They are there not only to help him, after all! The farmers continue to warn us about the priest Don Alessandro, who they say works for the Nazis and who would sell anything for money. And really, some evenings you can see Germans arriving at his home with cars and having dinner and doing business with him. It seems that there is at least some truth to Lieutenant Ubaldo's remarks.

George arrived in Bominaco, and together we went down to Caporciano for the meeting of different commanders, autonomous and otherwise. George told me he had a very interesting announcement to make. In the barn I could see Aurelio and Ugo and a group of people I didn't know. Ubaldo presented the orders and aspirations of the brigade based in Aquila: they wanted to get more weapons, carry out scattered small actions and be ready for the final attack when the Allies resumed their operations in our sector of the front. George asked to speak. He announced that he had made contact with a British captain who had parachuted in and was working in our area. George said he had explained the situation to the English officer — of the various groups operating in the area and their wish to link up and establish contact with the British. The British captain had decided to come to Opi and operate from there. George ran into

133

LUIGI FLEISCHMANN

him by pure chance. The Captain was sitting near the
fireplace in a house when George came in. He went to sit
by him and showed him his British passport. The captain,
who calls himself "Alfred," went out with him, and they
started to talk. The various commanders said they trusted
George completely in his dealings. Then Ubaldo reported
on the change in the captured artillery shells. With very
delicate "surgery," Ubaldo, who is an artillery officer, had
succeeded in adding a very thin steel spring to the shells'
detonator. By adding a very small plate, under a certain
amount of pressure, the shell would behave like a mine.
In the following days he would test one of them out. The
meeting ended.

I went to Opi. I was curious to know this Captain
"Alfred." We lay in a field under the spring sun with
George and the Russian. Alfred is thin and tall, with fair
hair, a red neck and blue eyes. He gives us the impression of
being very strong. He speaks very little, but knows Italian
quite well. He always keeps his eyes and his ears open
and on the alert. Above our heads flew four-engine Allied
bombers and the Russian looked up at them, smiling. He
likes to hear news about "his front," and looked at me
unbelieving when I showed him the situation on a map.
He couldn't believe that the Russians had already reached
the Romanian border and were positioned in front of
Lemberg in Poland. Then he laughed, looking jokingly at
the British captain, who didn't react, and said, "Cassino.
Ha! Ha! And the Russians advance!" He is a kind-hearted
man who talks all the time about his fields, his Russia, and
Stalin, and about the endless stones in the Abruzzi versus

134

FROM FIUME TO NAVELLI

the rich soil of the Ukraine. He makes fun of the old system of working the fields with donkeys as the Italian farmers do, and speaks of the "machines, machines" they use in the Ukraine.

In the evening, I quickly returned to Bominaco, because I had some news to bring to Ubaldo from Captain Alfred. It was dark, and about half way back I met four hobbling shadows walking in the dark. I felt terribly sorry for them. They were without doubt escaped British POWs. The first two were in quite bad shape, but the last one — walking some distance behind the others — looked absolutely terrible; not only completely tattered, wearing a kind of sack and holding a stick, but barefoot, his feet a mass of torn-up and bloody flesh from walking on all the stones and rocks. I do admire these Englishmen, with their courage and stubborn will, walking for months through all the mountains, in order not to be captured by the Germans. While nothing would happen to them, because they are soldiers they prefer to suffer hardships among the mountains than return to a POW camp. However, they really could not survive without the assistance and help of the Italian farmers who, at high personal risk, help them however they can.

I asked the first one, "Are you English?" He answered with a heavy British accent that even a deaf person could have distinguished, "No, we are Yugoslavs." They were frightened. Unfortunately I had no time to spend, otherwise I would have taken them personally to Opi to be treated and helped by the doctor, their fellow countryman. But I had to stick to my mission and go on. The last I saw of the men were four pitiful shadows, broken and tired, vanishing into the dark evening.

At home, we closed our "balance sheet" for the month of March with a rich dinner of chick peas and lentils, in good spirits and even merrily. Anyway, we figured that even if we were sad, things would not be any different — so what's the use of being down in the dumps?

A few days ago, Father swapped his best suit for 100 kilos of flour. He had to do it, otherwise there would not have been anything left to eat. But the bread continues to be black and the slices as thin as ever, because we don't know how long it must last.

April 1944

After quite a long time without any direct contact, Degen came up to Bominaco to visit us and told us that the secretary of Caporciano's town council had learned of our existence in Bominaco and wanted us to come to his office. He was a Republican fascist. Father walked down the three kilometers that same afternoon, and in the evening arrived back home, and told us the story. The man's name is Taddeo Lino. He is a schoolteacher and claimed he was only a fascist because he needed the job. He told Father he was aware of our situation and gave him an empty identity card on which he could write any name he wanted, and by which the secretary would issue him ration cards because he had heard of the arduous conditions under which we lived. Then he took leave from my father, promising that we had nothing to fear from him. In the evening we worked hard to "fill in" the identity card. From now on Father's name will be "Mr. Piccoli" from Mongrassano, near Cosenza. (We choose Cosenza because it is actually in the Allied occupied part of Italy, and thus impossible to check from our side.)

I went to Opi and was greatly relieved to find the four poor Englishmen I had met by chance. They had stopped there and the one with the wounded feet had been taken to the British doctor and received medical treatment. George took me to the cave where the four had taken shelter, and together we laughed at the way they told me that they were Yugoslavs. They recognized me at once. Now they are quite cheerful and well-fed. They want to leave again in a few days. Their names are Albert Rawles and Matthew Dotcherty. The one with the injured feet is Sergeant George, but I didn't catch his family name, or that of the fourth soldier, Charles. For the moment, a farmer — the widow Adele — brings them food, and lets them sleep at night in her cowshed. The four Englishmen had met Alfred too, who was very cold and evasive with them. But the cheerful and now completely healed Russian Afanacio immediately became their great friend. I was sorry that they intended to leave within a few days. Within a few hours, we also became good friends.

With the good weather back again, squadrons of Allied aircraft pass over us daily, and every morning on the Sirente long convoys of Flying Fortresses fly over, marked by the heavy deep hum of their four massive engines. We can hear many attacks on the main road but are unable to see anything because the road is 200 meters below us and blocked from our view by the mountains. Traffic on this road is scarce because the front line is still static.

Life in Bominaco during the past month has been stark and gloomy, and we plod on almost without noticing that spring has arrived. Our time and energies are occupied by our meager rations of thin slices of black bread and watery soups. With the arrival of the good weather, Mother now goes out into the fields to pick some edible grasses and plants, as some of the local women have demonstrated to her. All this is then cooked and eaten by us with the dignity of a prince eating a turkey — or something like it.

The two Italian officers who found shelter here left, but while trying to cross the battle line were betrayed by their guide and taken to Aquila by the Germans.

The Aloisio family I visit every evening are very nice. Like other people here, they try to help us in every way possible, but their means are limited, too. The only person that is always cheerful is Mr. Giosi. He's always humming some song and assuring us that "everything will end well." But Father is nervous and worried. Rumors are spreading that the Nazis are preparing a new search action, and that they don't trust the Italians anymore. For the time being they don't know where we are.

We received some news from Navelli. A unit of Italian fascist soldiers is now posted there, but they are unarmed. The Germans use them as workers under armed guards. The Germans have launched major defense projects in the area, building strongpoints on the mountains and digging bunkers all over the place. Now they are working on the Civitaretenga bottleneck. But these Italian soldiers, unwillingly called up, are deserting every day. Lieutenant Ubaldo has issued orders not to welcome them into any group, nor even to assist them.

Ubaldo and Antonio Conte told me that the test of the shell-mine went well. In order to avoid any suspicion, they did the test during an air raid, so the sound of the explosion was mixed with the explosions of the attack. They almost lost their lives. The mine went off very quickly and the cave in which it exploded almost fell in on their heads! Then some of the weapons of the Navelli group — which seems to be torn from within by intensive struggles between the communists and those of other opinions — arrived here, adding to the arms of the 2nd company.

My job is to be in Opi every afternoon for orders from Ubaldo and Captain Alfred. But for me it is more important to be with the former British prisoners and Afanacio the Russian. Over the last several days, George and Captain Alfred have been somewhere in the mountains most of the time, with signals and a radio transmitter no bigger than a small travel case. For the time being, the parachute drops are mostly boots and ammunition for the partisans. I knew that today George was on top of that mountain, communicating with two British aircraft circling in the sky, slowly and close up. I was at the bottom of a small valley surrounded by trees, lying on the grass and passing my time with my English friends and the Russian. I tried to convince them to stay in Opi — that they need not worry about becoming a burden to the farmers. (That was their main concern.) The partisans would help as much as possible. They were almost convinced, but still hesitated. They are very nice people. Albert and Matthew speak quite good Italian. They converse only in Italian with the Russian. They are soldiers, taken prisoner in Tobruk in 1942. Sergeant George is always silent and worried. He told me he was captured in Tunisia in December 1942. They all have a long record of wandering through the mountains and all of them highly praise the Italian farmers for their unselfish assistance. They said that they never knew that the Italians were so pro-Allies.

In the evening, George returned very optimistic. Every afternoon I go to Opi. It is now really pleasant to cross the narrow valley. Every other day I go to the command post of the 2nd company.

A British POW is sheltered in the house of the second-in-command, Antonio Conte. His name is Gerald O'Shea. He lives in a small room, shut off from the world for the last few months, but nevertheless he is very cheerful. His only fault is that being a good Irishman, he curses with every other word he utters. He is stocky with red hair and red skin, and wears a little locket with the image of S. Patrick on his shirt.

There is another man hidden in Antonio's house — an Italian policeman called Pasquale Lino. I could never distinguish between his first and family names. He always goes around with a gun in his pocket, even when he is near the Nazis. Lieutenant Ubaldo sends him on the more dangerous missions.

The Englishmen have decided, after many arguments,

to remain in Opi. Ubaldo has called among the partisans for a collection of clothes and food for them, but the burden still falls mostly on the widow Adele, with her three children, who cares for them in her house during the night. By day, they are in the fields. Afanacio is happy that his allies are to remain with him in Opi.

The British family living in Opi copes with the same difficulties that we face in Bominaco. The Degens are managing poorly as well, but Mrs. Degen has a very good business instinct and somehow copes with the farmers. We know absolutely nothing of the fate of the Billig family.

The Nazis continue to fortify the hills around Navelli and Civitaretenga. They have recruited hundreds of farmers for this work, because too many Italian fascists soldiers have chosen to desert.

Last night, for the first time, material was dropped for the partisans under the cover of night. The armed partisans waited in the narrow valley between Opi and Bominaco. After signaling with lamps, an airplane came in low and dropped something. The second drop was off-target, most of the supply falling into the next valley, Fontecchio, a low-laying area where the Germans took it all. The boots in the container dropped here have been given to the escaped POWs in Opi, who were happy to get very strong English army boots. Some signal rockets were dropped, too. Ubaldo took them. This first drop, a trial run, was not very successful. Alfred is always on the move with his radio transmitter to avoid his transmissions being intercepted and pinpointed by the Germans.

It is now Easter time. A few days ago, we Jews celebrated

a sad and dark Passover. Nobody can say that the black and scarce bread really took the place of *matzah*, but we tried to eat as little as possible.

On Easter, the priest Don Alessandro — considered by everybody to be a spy — went from house to house, blessing each home and receiving payment in eggs and other foodstuffs. When he arrived at our house, he entered and we let him do whatever he wanted. Then when we tried to give him some eggs in payment — what else could one do with a suspected spy? But he sent his assistant out of our house together with his basket, shut the door and then took ten eggs out from under his cassock. He put them on our table, saying he didn't need them, but we did. Then he left — leaving us totally astounded. If he took them out from under his cassock, it meant that this was preplanned. He must have come prepared to give them to us, and had already hidden them before he left his house!

Ubaldo wanted me to go to Navelli. So did my family, so I could look for some food. I traveled with a wagon — together with the foolish priest Don Beppe, who came to Bominaco out of pure curiosity. On board a wagon, the trip takes much less time. When I reached the plain of Navelli, I saw Germans and Italians performing some very unusual work along the main road: cutting down and taking away all the telephone and telegraph poles on both sides of the road. As we approached with the wagon, one of the soldiers from the signal corps still in Navelli looked at me, very surprised that I dared come back. So I entered Navelli as surreptitiously as I could. The next day I returned, walking all the way back on foot, reaching Bominaco with a bag full of chickpeas on my shoulder.

George arrived in Bominaco together with Alfred and Afanacio. While George went down to Caporciano for an hour, we accommodated the other two. This Russian is very nice, always cheerful. In Opi, he argued with the Englishmen, making them furious when he told them about the great Soviet victories, and making fun of the Allies because of the stationary situation on our front line. They made a bet. He wagered that the Russians would reach Berlin first; the Englishmen wagered that British forces would get there first. Afanacio, whose name they shortened to "Fanacio," insisted to the British that the cows in Russia have horns bigger than anywhere, saying "Russia, moo-moo. This…" — putting his hands on his head to demonstrate how big their horns are. He did the same in regard to Ukraine potatoes, which he purported are also "big like this," and that for Easter they slaughter pigs "big like this." The Englishmen made fun of his cows and potatoes and pigs. For Easter, the widow Adele cooked a nice dinner for the ex-POWs and I was a guest, too. They were all happy, and drank to the pending liberation. Let us hope.

When Captain Alfred speaks, something he rarely does, he always talks with a certain contempt of the Italians, rather than speaking of their generosity. He nicknames the Italians *Domani Dopodomani* in his strange English accent. He maintains that when one wants something to be done, the Italians always reply, "Tomorrow, or the day after tomorrow."

143

One day, I carried to Opi a bag full of clothing collected by the partisans for the British prisoners.

Life in Bominaco is always the same. With the ration cards with the fake names we sometimes get sugar, which we then solemnly add to the dirty water we call coffee.

A new problem has arisen: wood for cooking. So we have decided to become woodcutters. We went together for the first time with the Aloisio family and a donkey. We worked in the forest for a whole morning; I had to lead the donkey carrying the wood on his back. But the animal refused to go in the direction I wanted, so we parted ways. I was very angry. The donkey remained placid but unmoved…then returned to the village on its own. Everybody laughed at me.

This evening, Alfred came to us alone. Later, I accompanied him to the path to Opi. From this vantage point, near the ruined chapel, we could control the whole of Bominaco. Suddenly, from the road coming up to the hamlet we saw two German cars approaching. Alfred looked at his watch. It was 5:30 p.m. He looked at the cars entering Bominaco and at his watch again, and then said, "All right,"…and disappeared. I returned to the village and found everything in turmoil: the Nazis were searching everywhere! As I ran to the Aloisios, a car halted and Germans rushed out. It looked as though the Nazis were after the church. They were looking for a radio transmitter and for the priest. I ran down to join my family and we all fled to the next mountain. At one point, Livio paused and ran back to fetch the documents we forgot to take with us. We quickly climbed the mountain as darkness began to descend. We stopped at the summit, under the big cross of the chapel of S. Michele. I crawled to the point from where it was possible to see Bominaco and anybody who might have gone up to where we were hiding.

Hours after we arrived on the mount of S. Michele, the Germans below were still searching. It was quite cool, but the night was very clear. I wondered what they are looking for in little Bominaco…

In the middle of the night, we heard the German cars leaving. We abandoned our hiding place and went back down to the hamlet. There we met Anna Aloisio and her sister-in-law Olga, who were waiting for us.

We returned home feeling relieved, but this was the third search operation we had survived. How long would we succeed in evading being taken away?

This search was somewhat mysterious. They arrested Don Alessandro the priest — for spying it seems — quite ironic since it was known that he was working for the Germans. Michele Agrippa escaped by chance, jumping across walls and over ditches, when the Nazis came planning to arrest his father Don Ferdinando, who was playing cards with Servetto and Giosi. They thought he was a "British mayor." For almost the whole night, the Nazis searched the church looking for a radio transmitter but, as I well know, they were on the wrong trail.

When I related the story in Opi, I remembered how, a few minutes before the search started, Alfred looked at his watch saying, "All right." When I talked with George and Alfred, I asked them "if by any chance it was they who, in order to eliminate a German spy, told the Germans that the priest was working for the Allies." Alfred responded with a very thin smile — nothing more. Well, it could be that such doings are the mysterious workings of the British intelligence services, so I didn't ask any more questions.

From time to time, the former POWs are visited by Leo and the Scotsman Ben, who are always around and about. I suspect that they belong to the British intelligence services network that maintains contacts between the partisans and Alfred. They always are very reticent, talking only with Captain Alfred, never with other people.

Father is again nervous and worried because of the rumors Degen told us about Nazi plans for a new search operation. Our three Jewish families have survived so much, but now that our area is slowly becoming a German defense line, things are becoming all the more dangerous for us.

The food situation is about the same as before. But the beautiful weather and the noise of the Allied forces — planes that fly in long lines over us or over the Sirente daily — cheer us up. This is especially true for Mother, who has never lost her good humor during all these dark and dangerous months, even in the midst of the worst hardships and dangers. My brother Livio is a fountain of endless energy and good will. He lights the fire, chops the wood and somehow manages to find some of the rarest commodities. If we run out of soap, he appears the next day with soap. Where from, we never ask.

Father gave me our genuine documents and I brought them to Antonio Conte. He hid them somewhere, burying them in an iron box. Now our name is "Piccoli" and not Fleischmann anymore.

146

Aloisio's radio brings us good news, but always from the Eastern Front: the Russians are in Bessarabia. And the British? As always, they are still in Ortona, on the Majella, and at Anzio and Cassino.

Lieutenant Ubaldo told me that he got an order from brigade headquarters to move out with his group under the cover of night, march 30 kilometers carrying explosives and attack a bridge. But he refused to leave the area for such a long march with the entire group, and all its arms and ammunition, only to blow up a bridge. The brigade had other groups nearer the target, he argued. He added that this would always be his stance. The bridge in question is on the main road, leading from Avezzano to Aquila, at the foot of Mount Sirente.

18 APRIL 1944

In the morning, George Osmo-Morris and Albert Rawles arrived. They took me along with them on a mission. We had to walk a long way among the mountains to reach S. Benedetto in Perillis, about 20 kilometers away, in order to find out what had happened to some supplies wrongly dropped there by parachute, and to bring an order to the underground radio station in Rocca Pretura — quite a distance from here.

It was raining. I started the long march with the two Englishmen, splashing in the mud and walking through stony valleys and hills and up steep mountains I had never

147

seen before. Only George was armed with a handgun. We marched bent forward against the rain. Higher up in the mountains, the rain changed to an icy sleet, and the wind hit us with full force. It was a completely desolate and forbidding place, filled with stones and bushes, ravines and steep summits. A few kilometers ahead lay the German line, with its reinforced positions and barbed-wire obstacles. We had to try and evade them.

In a narrow valley, we unexpectedly met a column of fascist soldiers and mules carrying boxes. George fingered his gun, but they did not seem concerned about us. We went on. To evade the barbed-wire line, we climbed higher and higher up the mountainside. Suddenly, a sunray pierced the gray clouds and the rain, and we were able to see Navelli on our left — very small — down below us in the distance. We were walking at an altitude of about 1,000 meters. Despite our hobnailed boots, we constantly stumbled on the endless stones in our path, each of us walking silently, deeply immersed in his own thoughts.

At noon, we took a short rest, and then resumed our march. We had already been walking for four hours amongst the mountains. Then, all of a sudden S. Benedetto in Perillis appeared before our eyes. The village seemed strangely silent and quiet. Our suspicions were immediately aroused. Outside the village, we encountered an old woman. Realizing who we were, she warned us to flee. The Germans had blown up a house in which escaped Allied POWs had found shelter. Nevertheless we pressed forward, passing the demolished structure and heading for our rendezvous point. But we were in for an unpleasant surprise: nothing could be done about the dropped materials. The parachuted supplies had fallen into the hands of the Germans. Quickly, we left the village, walking in a westerly direction through ditches and over stones.

After another march of about an hour, we reached a place above Rocca Pretura. We had been instructed to bring Alfred's orders there. We started to go down into the small village, balanced on the steep slope of the mountain, when a partisan intercepted us, breathless, warning us not to enter the village. The Nazis were searching everywhere. They'd seized the radio transmitter and captured the whole team working with it. It was a total disaster! We retreated as quickly as possible, again cutting through the mountains towards the east.

It looked as though the Germans had decided to undermine the whole organization and its links with the British. Rocca Pretura was another major blow to the partisan cause, and we had accomplished nothing by our arduous trip.

We walked and walked. Our feet moved automatically, totally numb by that point. George smoked. Albert and I were depressed. Since early morning, for eight hours, we had been walking through the mountains. Some distance from Caporciano, fed up with the events of the day, we descended to the plain and continued along the road, but on the outskirts of the village we spied a German guard. The Englishmen didn't exactly look like Italian farmers, even dressed in rags as they were. We decided to pass anyway. The German soldier looked at us, George cheerfully said: "Good evening, comrade!" and we were through.

We told Ubaldo the bad news and left. Three more kilometers and I was home in Bominaco, but the two others had to walk for another hour before reaching Opi. I went to bed very tired after a nine-hour march with our nerves always on the alert. In both directions we had walked 34 kilometers through the mountains!

Once again there was a shortage of firewood and all of us — Father, Livio and I — had to go into the woods again to cut down some wood. We thought how happy we would all be if the only thing we were missing was firewood! Nevertheless, it was wonderful to walk in the woods early in the morning, wet with the fragrance of the dew. The sun rose slowly and the weather began to warm up. But there was not much in the Abruzzi woods — just small trees and bushes growing on the slopes of steep hills. We got to work, with the song of a cuckoo accompanying us as we toiled away. It could have been very picturesque had it not been for the arduous and dangerous situation, but we were quite cheerful this morning. Father and Livio vanished quickly into the green wood, and I could hear hacking noises and shouts. I had to gather the cut wood and carry it to the clearing, where we tied the kindling into bundles. At noon, the sun was high in the sky. Father and Livio came back, tired and sweaty. I was very tired, too. They hacked down the wood, but I had to collect it all, going up and down the slope. Later, we pulled the bundles like small baby carriages behind us. It's amazing how such very thin tree can be so heavy when cut down and gathered in a bundle! But we cheerfully lugged it all home, where a thick and smoking chick pea soup and some pasta awaited us. This time, for the first time in many months, we even had some salt thanks to "Mr. Piccoli's" ration cards.

Spring raises our spirits and we are cheerful all the time. The Aloisios and the Agrippas and others — especially Mrs. Giosi — think highly of us. They doubt whether under similar conditions, with their very lives in danger, they would have had the strength and strong spirit to go through all we have suffered. They believe the Jews are a very strong and stubborn race.

My daily visits to Opi are now such a routine that I don't mind at all walking two hours a day — one in each direction. The area is getting more beautiful every day and it cheers me up. In Opi, it is the same thing every day. After dealing with the different reports with Captain Alfred — to whom by the way, I gave a very nice drawing of the shooting down of the fighter plane in Navelli, and a caricature of pleasant times with them. The Russian is very amusing. Opi is now a kind of "transit site" for escaped Allied POWs, led by the clandestine "web" under the command of Captain Alfred. Yesterday, two more escapees arrived, one with two gunshot wounds in his head. They had been captured and taken away in a German vehicle. But one of them had a knife, wounded the German sentry, and both then jumped from the truck. The second fellow is South African. They were shot at but escaped, and two days later arrived here. Doctor Osmo-Morris took care of the wounded man. A member of Fontecchio's group found a place for the escapees in a little hamlet about a kilometer from Opi called Ripa di Fagnano. In Opi alone we have 11 Englishmen, including the Osmo-Morris family (and two escaped prisoners, from time to time), Ben and Leo, and one Russian — all this in a village of 160 inhabitants. The Italians help in every way possible. Luckily, Opi is a place "lost" in the middle of the mountains, across two valleys with no Germans around. For several days now, Captain Alfred has been very busy with his radio transmitter.

21 APRIL 1944

Today I was in Opi from early morning. Antonio Conte, Lieutenant Ubaldo and Aurelio from Caporciano and Navelli, had a meeting with the British Captain. Antonio Conte brought the English prisoner he had been sheltering in his house with him, so Gerald O'Shea finally met his fellow countrymen from Opi. He had come here to enjoy a "change of air." During the meeting, I sat in the little valley with Renato Osmo-Morris and the escaped POWs. We ate dinner on the grass.

In the afternoon, George and Alfred invited the partisan officers to witness an impressive spectacle. We climbed up to the square with them. From there one can see the beautiful green plain of S. Demetrio spread out below, and about 10 kilometers to the far side lies the small airport of Montecchio, which the Germans have turned into a big storage depot for ammunition and fuel. It is so well camouflaged that Captain Alfred discovered it only by chance, with the help of a partisan. At 3 in the afternoon, as we stood there taking in the scenery, two groups of fighter bombers approached and, directed via radio by Alfred, swept down on the target, which could clearly be seen from where we were positioned.

Within minutes, all hell broke loose: diving aircraft, explosions, anti- aircraft fire and then a huge explosion followed by a great column of fire. The whole dump was blown up and burned in a series of endless explosions. George shook hands with everyone, laughing wildly. Captain Alfred bid us farewell and retired with his radio set to a nearby mountain to evade German magnetic interception. We all left very pleased.

Father's lessons continue, and he is very happy with his "pupils." It is a great relief and diversion for him because besides the lessons, they all talk for hours about anything and everything. Professor Servetto, who is an architecture teacher in Aquila, wanted to see my drawings. As he looked at them, he said they were very nice and dubbed me "Michelangiolic." Quite an exaggeration, of course!

Bominaco is without a priest. The farmers are angry because they discovered that before his arrest, Don Alessandro had sold some of the church's gold.

The Germans are hard at work building their defenses on the surrounding mountains. But their biggest efforts are invested in the narrow bottleneck of Civitaretenga down in the plain, as well as on Mount S. Erasmo, a very dreary peak directly to our south, some three kilometers from Bominaco.

Several times during the week I visit Caporciano — always at Ubaldo's place. We are in the midst of reorganization and preparation in expectation of some action come spring. A compromise agreement has been reached with Bruno, the communist committee leader of the underground C.L.N. (Committee of National Liberation).

I was standing near the window, gazing out. Father, Mother and Livio were at the Aloisios' house, but I didn't know why. Signor Mario was suffering from a terrible toothache but that couldn't have been the reason for their visit. Suddenly, through the window, I saw a car full of Germans making its way up the winding road to Bominaco. Another search operation? I ran out quickly, armed with my iron-tipped stick — my "constant companion" in the past few months — come what may. I reached the top of Mount S. Michele. There I stopped to look down, and saw Germans climbing the same path I'd taken. I quickly ran down another way and climbed up another hill, wandering around like this for two hours. I had no idea where I could join up with the partisans, so I cut through the mountains and arrived in Caporciano in time to see the Germans coming down from Bominaco in a cloud of dust. What took them so long? And what about my family?

Lino is always present at Antonio Conte's house. He called Antonio and told him that he knew what had happened in Bominaco. The Germans had come to search for Jews, but hadn't found anybody. I ran up. My family — still very shaken — told me what had happened. They had had no time to grasp what was happening and escape in time. The Germans had already sealed and blocked the entire hamlet, and were questioning the Italian farmers in their houses: "Any Jews here? Any refugees?" Everyone answered that they didn't know what Jews looked like, and that nobody was there. My family was sitting in a room at Aloisios', unable to move, while Mario Aloisio paced back and forth in the room yelling at the top of his lungs because his tooth had swollen his whole face. The Germans started a house-to-house search and soon arrived at the Aloisios' place. Advocate Santucci was sitting at a table together with my father. The Germans asked if "anybody knew a man called Fleischmann, with glasses and mustache who was wanted and also a Jew." Father and the rest sat petrified, glued to their chairs. With tremendous aplomb, Advocate Santucci looked at Father and retorted, "What do you want! This man here also wears glasses and has a mustache, but he is not Jewish and his name is Piccoli!" Throughout the search, Mario Aloisio continued to yell in pain and pace up and down the room. After searching for some time, the Germans finally left the hamlet empty handed, disgusted at having wasted their time.

This was one of the most perilous encounters we had had to date, but the "hand of fate" seems to have led us once more to safety.

MAY 1944

I continue my visits to Opi. The four Englishmen are now so familiar with their surroundings, it as if they have always been part of the landscape. Afanacio the Russian talks constantly about the potatoes and the fields in the Ukraine, and the slowness of the Allied war operation. But the English smile and are merely amused. The widow Adele makes great efforts to help these four fugitives, who are all healthy blokes with big appetites. But they understand the difficult situation well, and help in the fields and manage somehow. The Osmo-Morris' live as usual. Now, with the nice weather, the doctor walks a lot with his little dog, Lilla. A few days ago, the doctor fell asleep very contented under a tree and woke up with a snake on his shoulder looking at him in the face! But the snake slithered away leaving the doctor unharmed.

The weather is getting nicer all the time. The trees are already green and the fields are blooming. One can see how the weather is changing. The sky is blue and calm and the weather is very mild. Only in the afternoon — something I noticed already last year — clouds from east to west partly cover the skies. From early morning until evening, endless columns of Allied aircraft fill the skies with the hum of their engines, but the front line is still silent and static. The Germans are investing tremendous energies in their fortifications. They dig trenches and foxholes and, with the help of explosives, are erecting strongpoints and barriers as if the battle will start any moment.

Captain Alfred is quite worried because the Germans have started a large repressive action against partisan groups, and it seems that our area will be their next objective. There are rumors that a great search action will soon start in the two valleys. For some time, he hasn't dared operate the radio transmitter, because he believes the Germans are "sounding out" the area. They must be very cautious. The fuel and ammunition dump at Montecchio was too well-camouflaged in order to be spotted and attacked by chance by Allied planes flying over. But the escaped prisoners in Opi haven't asked too many questions. That should be Alfred's job. The two escaped prisoners sheltered in Ripa di Fagnano have been added to the group, and everybody helps out.

My family is the same. They are very nervous. It is now May, the weather is warming up but we are in the same situation as three, four or five months ago. On top of everything, our two small rooms have been invaded by swarms of flies.

I have become very friendly with Michele Agrippa, a very nice boy. His elder brother crossed the front line in March, and now he is in the Italian liberation army and undoubtedly waiting to return to Bominaco as a liberator. We would like to cross the fighting line too, if possible. Father has decided to try this option, because he fears that worse things are in store for us here. Through partisan channels, I have learned where and how I can find the group of guides who smuggle British intelligence officers across the battle line. The group is led by a "red" partisan by the name of Corpi, as well as others. But we have been warned that it is dangerous now, in the springtime, because the Germans are on the alert, and crossing the Majella is a terrible undertaking. So slowly we relinquish this idea — raised only due to growing trepidation over the increasingly difficult situation we now find ourselves in since moving to Bominaco.

6 MAY 1944

In answer to the rumors of a repressive search action, Lieutenant Ubaldo and the 2nd company attacked the main road by night. The shell-mines worked well, and two German trucks were blown up with their crews and cargo with deafening explosions.

It seems that the Nazis have sent some spies into the vicinity with orders to infiltrate the partisan organization. A few days ago, a woman appeared at Antonio Conte's house. By chance, he was at home. The woman wanted to know how she could join the partisan unit. Antonio Conte played innocent, answering coolly that he would ignore her dangerous question, and she left.

I went for a meeting with Alfred and George to Ubaldo's command post and headquarters of the 2nd company. Various items were on the agenda. The British captain explained that an air supply would be parachuted only if the company conducted some big and important attack. He pointed out the possibility of an assault on Civitaretenga, where the Germans had stockpiled large amounts of explosives and tools for their work in a church, adding that in the same action it would also be possible to blow up the German strongpoints. Ubaldo objected, saying that he would not carry out such an action — not because he is not able to do it, but because the German reprisals would be terrible and not directed against the partisans but against the civilians in Caporciano and Civitaretenga. Captain Alfred was not very happy to hear this, but the sides agreed to leave things as they were. Ubaldo was firm in his decision to continue with surprise attacks on German convoys and, for the time being, not take part in actions like those proposed by Alfred. Ubaldo told me that all the "Mitra" sub-machine guns now have magazines — the fruit of the labors of the village blacksmith — and they all work well.

Back to woodcutting! We have gotten used to this work by now, but we sweat a lot because it is getting hot. The views are more beautiful now in the woods, at least for me. We work hard — our labors accented by our chopping noises and shouts. Then we rest — wet with perspiration — under a blue sky, while flies and other insects hum and buzz around us in the muggy air, annoying us by landing on our flushed faces. But the hardest part is pulling all the felled kindling down the hill and then up another steep hill to the house. Mother is working hard, too, carrying the water or walking for a mile down to a narrow valley where there is a spring to wash the few things we still own because we have constantly had to trade more and more of our belongings to obtain some food. A few days ago, Mother had to sell her gold watch to a rich farmer's wife in Navelli. She had to go all the way there to trade it for oil and fat. The farmers, even with their good intentions, have to take care of the future of their livelihoods. Everybody can sense that the war is destined to cut through these fields. There is no guarantee for the growing crops under such conditions, so the farmers are concealing and storing everything they possess.

Lieutenant Ubaldo stopped at our house on his way to Opi. Father talked to him about our situation. Rather desperate, he told Ubaldo that he is tired of it all…and who knows how long we will have to wait for some change? Ubaldo encouraged him, promising Father that in two days the Italian front would open up again. He said he knew that because of Alfred's orders on his radio and news that in the coming days supplies would be dropped by air to help the partisans carry out attacks coordinated with the upcoming Allied offensive.

I now stay in Opi longer than in Bominaco. Together with "my Englishmen" and Afanacio, we observed an Allied air attack on a German column marching near S. Demetrio. There was a lot of noise and it was a very interesting spectacle, but because of the distance we were unable to see the effect.

The British, and especially Alfred and Matthew, are very irritated with the Italians. They noticed that when the Italian farmers see some very effective air raids, they say that the pilots of the fighter-bombers must certainly be Italians fighting on the Allied side, and when the attack is not very successful, they decide that the pilots must be British! The ex-POWs make fun of these fantasies, and tell them stories about the war against the Italian army in the Western Desert (Egypt).

9 MAY 1944

In the evening, while mother was returning from the fountain with a bucket full of water, a man who didn't look Italian accosted her. He was wearing glasses and had a rucksack on his back. He started to speak. "You're from Fiume, aren't you?" Then he asked Mario Aloisio for some information about partisans. When I heard about this, I took off in the darkness to the partisan headquarters down in Caporciano and told them about the stranger. We all suspect he is a Nazi spy. Many strangers wander about in these parts, saying they are Slavs. This one told the same story. We remember what happened to Antonio Conte. I suggested that Ubaldo come to Bominaco and "eliminate" the suspicious visitor. After thinking for a while, Ubaldo replied, "No. If the man *is* a Gestapo agent and was sent here on a mission, and he disappears while he's here, then the Nazis will start looking for him. A person doesn't just disappear into thin air. So for the moment it is better to leave him where he is." He advised me to remain calm, and after drinking some wine I returned to Bominaco by moonlight. Because of the wine, I was a bit tipsy and at every shadow cast by the curbstones, imagined a black corpse lying on the white road.

In Bominaco, the Aloisios provided accommodation for the suspicious man. He told them he would leave the next morning. On the radio we heard that the Soviets have liberated Sevastopol.

10 MAY 1944

Hurrah! The 5th and 8th Allied armies are attacking on

a broad front running from Cassino along the Garigliano River, all the way to the Tirrenian Sea. The attack must be very forceful! So the tip that Ubaldo and Captain Alfred gave us about pending events must be true. After lunch, I ran the three kilometers to Opi as fast as possible to bring the good news to the Englishmen. Over my head, Allied bomber formations were met by German anti-aircraft fire on the Sirente and at Rocca di Mezzo, and the noise of explosions accompanied me along the way.

Now again our hopes are high for the outcome of this great offensive. We are certain that our part of the front will soon start to move, too. At home we are in good spirits.

We hope and pray that maybe now the Republican fascist police will stop looking for us after our "disappearing act" three months ago. But the Germans will certainly not give up. Mr. Giosi is very cheerful. He believes that very soon he will be able to return to Napoli. At the English-German classes they follow the beginning of this attack more than the grammar lessons! But all this doesn't ease our situation. We still have to cut firewood regularly.

One of the negative aspects of living in our house here in Bominaco is that there is no toilet or nearby stable. So we use a bucket. When it is full at night, Mother and I go out into a small valley to empty its stinking and disgusting contents into a cave. There is no other way. Livio faithfully mends Father's shoes, really turning this task into a "work of art." But our main course at lunch still consists of chickpeas and edible grass, black bread and, from time to time, some pasta.

12 MAY 1944

Ubaldo's 2nd company launched another attack by night against a German horse-drawn convoy. It seems that the wooden carriages are more resistant than trucks. They don't completely fall apart. Up until now, four German soldiers have been killed and accounted for. The shell-mines function very well — like real mines — all thanks to Ubaldo's ingenuity.

At Opi, the British POWs await my arrival every afternoon to hear the latest news about the battle. But there is little news to report now. The Allies have made very few advances, as they slowly break down the so-called "Gustav" line. I wonder why it is called "Gustav"?

I rarely see Alfred lately. Together with George, he wanders about in the mountains doing who knows what. In the afternoon, while on my way to Opi, I was terrified to see that same suspicious man who accosted mother just a few days ago walking in the fields. I made a long detour in order not to meet him.

While in Caporciano, I observed that many Germans are here, too. I have come to know the family of Antonio Conte's brother — a well-to-do family that owns the store where we buy our rations with the fake ration-cards. Mr. Degen has introduced me to Mrs. Conte, a very nice woman.

It is spring and all the Italian farmers are busy now in their fields. They await their liberation and follow the new offensive with great interest. The village is now full of Nazis, climbing up the mountains with maps and optical instruments. These are the German alpine troops checking out the area where they may soon be fighting.

How we would like to be in that situation…as soon as possible! But down below, the Majella is still quiet; no one has started to move in this area yet.

16 MAY 1944

Today I brought good news with me to Opi. Cassino is occupied, as is Gaeta, and the whole Garigliano line has been broken through at Esperia by French and American forces! We all joyfully drink a toast! Captain Alfred asks me to report two things to Ubaldo: first, a very important supply drop for the partisans will be carried out in the next few days; and second, the Germans are building up their forces against us in this area and there is a strong possibility that soon there will be a very strong German action against our groups. They don't want any possible trouble now on their rear. Ubaldo should be on the alert.

18 MAY 1944

Under Lieutenant Ubaldo, the 2nd company carries out an attack with automatic weapons against a German convoy between S. Pio and Castelnuovo, some four or five kilometers north of Caporciano. But Ubaldo told me this attack was really carried out to test the homemade "Mitra" magazines, which worked very well. He asked me to report to Captain Alfred to be on alert.

In Bominaco, we are now very tense, eagerly waiting for the latest news, just as we did five months ago in that dark and sad December. But this time we are convinced that this new Allied offensive will break through, and not stop a mere few kilometers after breaching the German lines. The Anzio beachhead is not moving for the moment.

The Aloisios are happy about the news as well. They are happy for us, and talk about the day when we will be free and not persecuted any more, or hunted like rabid dogs.

Above our heads endless formations of airplanes hit anything and everything in the vicinity — bridges, roads and other targets — perhaps in preparation for the next attack in our area.

I have heard very little from Navelli. The Germans have confiscated all the fields between Navelli and the narrow bottleneck of Civitaretenga, and are filling them with hundreds of mines of every kind. They also string barbed wire obstacles and dig huge foxholes.

Bominaco is in turmoil: the Germans have confiscated the cattle. Are we already at the plundering stage? I can hear the shouts of angry farmers and Nazis orders being barked out, all mixed with the mooing of cattle. The Nazis departed with seven cows, so desperately needed in the village. Those reluctant to comply were threatened with execution. The Germans also rounded up hundreds of donkeys. Bominaco too, has to "deliver" its livestock for the fortification works being carried out on the surrounding hills. The farmers, enraged by the German confiscation of their livestock, demanded some action by the partisans. But Ubaldo is unwilling to get mixed up in this. It could lead to unnecessary reprisals.

While Father was giving a lesson to Santucci, the Servetto girls and Michele Agrippa at the Servettos', some Germans suddenly entered the house. With the help of a Tyrolean interpreter they demanded the radio set, citing some "high orders." But this order didn't exist any more, and it was clear that they simply wanted the radio for themselves — perhaps as a present to take to Germany. Servetto and Agrippa were compelled to give up their radio sets, leaving us with the one radio at the Aloisios' to hear the news.

While on my way to Opi, some of the farmers stopped me and gave me some of the nice ripe cherries they were picking. I ate as much as I was able, for my stomach is not always full on our diet of lentils, and brought the rest home. In Opi, I related the daily news of the slowly advancing front. The Englishmen relished with pleasure how Afanacio had to "defend his country's honor" by saying something about the cherries, too. He explained to the four Englishmen that in the Ukraine the cherries were — "big, big, big" — his hands demonstrating how big they are — "like melons!"

Captain Alfred wished me to report to Ubaldo that the day after tomorrow, Sunday, will be the day of the long awaited airdrop of supplies for the partisans. At night, they carried out another attack, blowing up a car.

21 May 1944

Catastrophe! About noon, Leo and Ben arrived at our house, very shaken. What happened? When I heard, my head began to spin. During the night, the Germans attacked Opi and captured Captain Alfred, the British family and George Osmo-Morris. Leo and Ben were saved by miracle. They and the Russian were sleeping in George's room when suddenly the Germans entered with guns and flashlights in their hands. They apprehended George, who put up no resistance. Then the Germans turned the flashlights on their faces, but since their orders were to arrest only George in that house, they left Leo and Ben alone. The moment the Germans left, they jumped out the windows together with Afanacio and the other four escaped POWs, and ran for the woods. I was quite shaken and frightened, and so were they. They warned me not to go to Opi, because the Germans were looking for me. They wanted "a certain Luigi who speaks seven languages (!?)." I was panic-stricken when I heard this and so was my family. The two Englishmen departed for the mountains. What a disaster! If Leo and Ben had not warned me, I would have gone unknowingly to Opi for the airdrop, and fallen into the trap.

But what was I waiting for? As quickly as possible I ran down to Caporciano. Pale and shaken, I entered the room of Lieutenant Ubaldo (I can imagine how I looked to him…) and informed him that Captain Alfred had been captured, as well as George and his family. Ubaldo turned pale. But I had barely updated him when Antonio Conte, also shaken, ran in, followed by Bruno from Navelli, dirty and soaked with sweat. Last night, the Germans hit the partisans of the Navelli C.L.N. as well, capturing Aurelio, Ugo Umberto and Iginio. We were all paralyzed with shock. When I told Antonio and Bruno what had happened in Opi, they were almost panic-stricken. Bruno told us that the evening before, the four were approached by two young women who told them they were British paratroopers. They agreed to meet that night at Settimio's Inn. When the four of them, led by Aurelio, entered the room, the two women — guns in hand, were waiting for them with other Germans, and they were caught. They were taken to the house of the signal unit. The Germans have been beating them for the past few nights and one can hear their screams all over Navelli. The village is terrorized. Bruno escaped, but he is wanted too, and the whole Navelli C.L.N. group has been forced to disband by this sudden German strike. Now we are really in dire straits. Lieutenant Ubaldo summed it up, saying that the two strikes were almost a lethal blow to the partisan cause. Now that Alfred's leadership is gone — and who knows if he is still alive — the 2nd company must carry on the struggle. Then he spoke about my personal situation. Since, for obvious reasons, he had to change his base of operation for another area and a different partisan group, he said I should go with him. I was to return in the evening to leave with him.

I returned to Bominaco completely shaken. I didn't tell my family what happened in Navelli. For the time being, it is better that way. The widow Adele assured me in a message from Opi that the British and the Russian were safe, but the Germans were looking for me. They knew my name because they had found the drawing I had made for Captain Alfred, and it was signed, as are all my drawings.

I had to disappear. Mother prepared something for me to take along. I burned Alfred's caricature and the partisan newspapers in the house and, with nightfall, returned to Ubaldo's place. At Antonio Conte's house I tried to make Gerald O'Shea understand how critical the situation was. The Irishman couldn't comprehend that if the Germans caught me, they would shoot me. "Yes, killed indeed," he said, unbelieving. He thinks that the Germans behave in war like the British.

Night of 21 May 1944

In the darkness, Ubaldo and I descended to a friendly house at the foot of Caporciano. We were ready; I carried my stick-weapon, but was quite tense. We stopped at the house and the Lieutenant told me that in the last few hours his personal situation had changed, too. The Nazis were looking for him — the *Perugino* — as well. They were determined to root out the various resistance groups, and now their objective was the 2nd company. They were searching Caporciano. That was the reason we had to wait at the house for a signal that would allow us to cross the German search parties without being detected. Suddenly, our hearts stopped. On the stones outside we heard steps and the noise of weapons. The Germans! We turned off the light and Ubaldo grabbed his gun. They halted outside, but after some exchange of words I couldn't understand, departed. After five minutes of suspense, we got the signal. Ubaldo and I rushed out into the dark night.

We walked quickly, bent over in the shadows of the bushes. I was breathing so heavily that Ubaldo told me to breath with my mouth open so as to make less noise. In the early morning, the 2nd company under Antonio Conte was due to slip out into another area, too. We had to reach a place quite far away — a deep wood on a mountain on the other side of the valley. We walked with heavy steps, trudging through the muddy fields, and went down into the plain. We could spot the main road about a mile from us. It was filled with marching Germans on their way to the front line.

Unfortunately for us, the British air force was shooting flares exactly over our heads, which lit up the entire area from time to time with a strong blue-white flash, compelling us to hit the ground and lay low to avoid being spotted. I was thinking about Bominaco and what if the Germans should look for me there, hoping against hope that nothing would happen to my family. Boom! The airplanes dropped some bombs, and again lit up the night with rockets. We quickly crossed the plain. After ten minutes, we reached a small church in the middle of the plain that had been destroyed. We stopped to rest and wait for the British attack to subside so we could proceed under the cover of darkness. I had never been there. It looked black and gloomy, but this assessment could have been subjective — reflecting my gloomy feelings of being pursued.

After another half hour of walking, we began to climb

the stony hillside. Another hour of pushing forward at a fast pace and we entered the woods. Suddenly, dark shapes covered with black blankets spring up from the ground — the partisan sentries. We were escorted inside the woods to another dark blanket with a partisan rolled inside. Thus, we were "handed" from sentry to sentry until we reached a hut of stone and straw. Inside, we met the leader of another group, Captain Giovanni Aloisi and Bruno — back again from Navelli, twelve kilometers distance from where we stood. He would hide us in the hut. He told us that they were still torturing the four captured men, but they still hadn't talked. One who behaved very well was my friend, Iginio Quintilio, who was my age. Because he was the youngest, the Nazis believed he would break easily. But it seemed they were wrong. Yet, we all wondered how long they would be able to hold on.

In Opi, the Germans blew up the house where the British lived. All these events, as well as Alfred's capture, had left a deep impression on the leaders of the various groups, but Ubaldo thought that nevertheless we would manage. The other partisans returned to their positions, and Ubaldo, Bruno and I fell asleep on the straw, while some mice tried to "attack" my boots. I was overwhelmed by a mixture of emotions.

22 MAY 1944

The hut in which we were hiding was very small and our

heads bumped the ceiling. In a corner there was a well with water. We washed up. The sun was very hot, even in the early morning. To feel more secure, we left the hut and lay under the surrounding trees. Up in the clear sky, a formation of Flying Fortresses, shining like mirrors in the sun, passed over, suddenly testing their weapons with a burst of fire, before attacking. Towards noon, Antonio Conte appeared and reported that the group had taken up positions in the woods without any incident. He had some good news for me: nothing had happened yet in Bominaco. The Germans had not searched there. They had even relinquished their siege of Opi. He also brought me a new fake identity card with a picture and authorized stamp. Thus, I learn that my name now is "Angelo Matteucci," my mother is "Maria," and I was born in Campana (Fontecchio) in 1929! Very well. Antonio Conte told us that everybody in the group was very much on edge. In the evening, Captain Giovanni Aloisi arrived to discuss some problems with Ubaldo and Bruno.

We went to sleep, still edgy and anxious. As we fell asleep, the usual Allied nighttime air raids continued outside with their flare rockets and falling bombs. But in the woods everything was silent.

23 MAY 1944

Bruno left the woods, escorted by partisan guides part of the way. His objective: a dangerous mission in Navelli. He had to find out what was happening, and if anything from the hidden weapons could be saved.

I felt quite down. At least here among the partisans I felt more secure, but I thought about my family in Bominaco. At noon, we walked for about 20 minutes and settled down under some Acacia trees to eat a good lunch brought by Antonio Conte and another partisan: a very good *pastasciutta*.[20] He brought news from the battle as well: the Allies were advancing and, after breaking the Cassino line, were now assaulting the "Hitler Line," and have also taken Terracina. But their advance is slow, and in our area they are still not moving at all.

In the evening, Bruno returned from Navelli, dead tired. He had to march through the mountains to evade the Germans. Nothing had changed there. The Nazis were still torturing Aurelio, Ugo, Lieutenant Umberto and Iginio Quintilio. But they remain silent. Bruno asked a woman he knew to try and get permission to talk to them. The visit was granted. Aurelio told her, "Nobody should fear anything, I won't talk." The woman described how all four have swollen heads because of the beatings, and lay on the floor in pain, unable to move. Our blood freezes when we think of the possibility of getting caught.

20 Italian dish, literally "dry pasta," meaning fresh pasta without sauce.

24 MAY 1944

Bruno decided to leave the shelter of the woods and return to Navelli. He says that his place is there, not in a hiding place. The weather is turning bad. For the last few days it has been exceedingly hot, and in the afternoon it started to rain heavily, but only for a short time. Later, after the rain stopped, I sat glumly on the grass outside the hut, gazing at the opposite end of the valley where, among the low clouds and the fog, I could discern the far-off outlines of the tower of Bominaco.

The commanders met in the hut. Lieutenant Ubaldo and Captain Aloisi decided to conduct a night attack on the main highway with the 2nd company and part of Aloisi's group. Under the cover of night, leaving directly from the hut, they attacked a German convoy. There were three explosions. Three trucks were hit, followed by an exchange of fire. That was all.

The mice must have a very strong appetite if they continue to try to gnaw at my boots while I sleep on the straw. But the boots are hobnailed and I don't believe mice can eat iron.

25 MAY 1944

Another day has passed here in the woods, at this hut. Ubaldo was pleased with the night attack. Indeed, from a certain vantage point in the woods, one can see the three destroyed German trucks down in the valley on the road. There were three dead as well — two of them in an ambulance which also blew up, and now lays overturned near the ditch at the side of the road.

Ubaldo has decided to move again with his company — this time to the other side of the valley in the direction of Caporciano. He will march by night. I have to remain here alone, for the other unit is moving out as well. This is the rule: after an attack, you have to move on. But I have to remain here alone in the woods at the hut until they tell me to leave. To make the waiting easier for me, Captain Giovanni Aloisi brought me a thick book –*The Will* — a novel by an author called Hutchinson. So I passed the night alone in the hut and, with the help of a small oil lamp, finished reading the entire book. My only fear was that while I slept I would get hit by one of the flares from those nighttime bombing raids.

26 MAY 1944

It was a very hot day, while the "usual" Allied aircraft continued to raid targets in the area. I got very bored being alone. I hadn't the slightest notion where everyone had gone.

At noon, I became alarmed. Down at the foot of the hill at the edge of the woods were Germans — combing the area after the attack! There was a German armored car with camouflage colors. There were some soldiers in the car and some walking behind it. They crossed the fields between the village of S. Pio delle Camere and the destroyed church on my left. I feared they might spot the hut and climb up to check it out. I beat a hasty retreat, hiding deep in the brush, sweating and cursing the flies and ants that annoyed me.

In the evening, Captain Aloisi returned: I was to leave and return to Bominaco or Caporciano, again serving as a liaison together with the policeman Lino. At dusk, rucksack on my back and stick-weapon in hand, I descended the mountain and crossed the plain. I passed not far from the destroyed cars, and got a whiff of the stench of the German corpses — still there rotting in the heat of the day. I reached Caporciano in the middle of the night and went straight to Antonio Conte's house. He was in, busy forging identity cards together with two other persons whom I didn't know.

Later that night, back again in Bominaco, my family welcomed me, without ceremony. They had had a very difficult time because of me, while I had to flee. They were constantly on the alert, but fortunately the Nazis didn't come. That night, Father stayed up all night near the window on guard, so I could sleep soundly.

27 MAY 1944

The Allied radio announced that the Americans were in Frosinone and the forces in the Anzio beachhead had begun their attack. Even the "Hitler Line" was falling to pieces. But on the hills and mountains around here, the Germans go on with their fortification work. All the fields down in Navelli have already been mined and closed.

Livio brought a bad piece of news: there is an order to arrest...Giosi. The police documents say he gave shelter to an Allied spy by the name of "Fleischmann." Giosi was half-crazy with fear. We ran down to Caporciano and met the Degens. They, too, were panic-stricken: the *Carabinieri* officer had told them that the Germans had made up their mind to be "finished and done with us" and plan to search for us again, this time more seriously. He, the police officer, would have to go with them on this manhunt, so he begged us to run away. We were terror-stricken again. We were perhaps five minutes from being liberated and still had to go through yet another ordeal. We really will have earned our liberation, if we have the luck to reach that day! The Degen family escaped from Caporciano. In Bominaco, Giosi was at a loss and didn't know what to do. We had to leave the house, and Aloisio offered us some room for our things. We quickly carried them over to their place. The wanted partisan commander from Fontecchio had been hiding in the shelter in his home ever since his group had been dispersed. He is called "Barbetta." I do not know anything else about him.

The Aloisio family gave shelter to my mother and Livio. Father and I went to Caporciano to hide in the house of Natale Conte. He is Antonio's brother, and though the relationship between the two brothers is very bad, the two made the arrangements to hide us — who knows for how long?! Through Lino, I let the group know that I was sorry not to be able to fulfill my duty for the time being, but I had to remain hidden together with my father.

28 May 1944

Natale Conte's family are really kind people. The head of the family is a very good man, a former socialist persecuted for his political views. He has two daughters, Jole and Luigina, both students.

For most of the day we lay on the flat roof, because the Contes always get a lot of visitors and many of the German soldiers posted in Caporciano visit the house, as well. But in the evening we had a plentiful dinner in the dining room of the house. Lino was there too, and through him I always have contact with the group. For the time being they are inactive again, but have been ordered to be ready for the final attack in about two weeks. Lino also brought us news, not only for me, but for Father and the Contes as well. The group has a radio, and in the evening they connect it to some power source, illegally listening to the news of the battle.

30 May 1944

Mr. Giosi came to Caporciano today to tell us what had

happened in Bominaco. The Germans came to search for us, but of course they could not find anybody. Things went easy for him, despite apprehensions. Since the Germans didn't find what they came for, they left him in peace. Giosi is of the opinion that a spy led the Germans to us and to him, and he is convinced that the informer is Cannata the painter who is still in Navelli. Giosi believes that Cannata passed on this tip through the command post of the fascist troops in Navelli. He is certain it could not be any other person. Only Cannata — painter and informer.

31 MAY 1944

It is now five days since we have been hiding in the house of Natale Conte. Time goes by very slowly. We hear many explosions. The Germans are feverishly setting off explosions to prepare positions for their defense line. We hope that all these endeavors will soon be put to the test, and the war will finally arrive in our area. At least personally we would be more secure.

Mrs. Anna Aloisio came down from Bominaco to bring us news from Mother and Livio. They are well and calm. The Germans did not look for them in the house.

In the evening Lino brought us the latest news. The Allies are now advancing swiftly; they have occupied Valmontone, linked up with the force coming out from Anzio, and then marched on Velletri. It looks as though the Allied pressure is spreading like a flood, and the

Germans are unable to stop the flow. But here, still nothing moves.

In the evening, the German officer in charge of Caporciano came to visit the Conte family. His name is Zimmermann. They didn't want him here at all, but still had to welcome him — especially now that we were hiding in their house! Stretched out on the roof of the terrace where they were all sitting, we were able to listen to him talk. The German officer was angry, speaking badly of "the Jews." He swore he would kill them with his own hands, if he could find any of them. Suddenly I moved, and my boots scratched the roof. The German asked, "What's that noise?" Jole ran up to the roof and whispered to me to take off my boots, then returned downstairs saying that it must have been a mouse.

June 1944

Stretched on the roof of Natale Conte's house, Father and I read and discuss different things to pass the time. From the command in Caporciano as well as from Ubaldo we have gotten word from Lino not to move yet. Father and I even manage to joke about out predicament. From the documents we have it appears that we are not even related. In fact, we don't even know each other! My name is "Angelo Matteucci" and this man hiding with me is called "Giulio Piccoli." Who knows who those Fleischmanns are that the Germans are after? We also think about the Osmo-

Morris'. Who knows where the Germans took them? As for the ex-POWs in Opi and the Russian, I know they are hiding in the forest near Opi and are all okay.

The sun is blazing down on us and it is already quite hot. Airplanes soar over our heads! British fighter-bombers attack. They dive to hit a German column marching near their strongpoint and the minefields of Civitaretenga. One of the planes turns and descends down over our heads and we can see two little black specks falling down from under his wings with a shriek. (The angle from which we view this is a sign that they are not falling *on* us.) Unfortunately, they explode with a bang on the side of the main road.

Our part of the front starts to move, as well. The British proceed quickly in the direction of the Pescara River valley and Sulmona. At last! Lino brought me the news that the partisans of the 2nd company got the order to be ready to move out on short notice, and I must remain here — in hiding!

2 JUNE 1944

We follow the news impatiently. We would like to leave but we can't. We have to hide until the Germans are so busy in our area they will not have time to think about hunting down wretched Jews! The Allies are already in Velletri, and from Cassino spread out to the northeast, towards the Abruzzi, Sora and Avezzano. From the roof of the house we are able to see, with growing trepidation, the long lines of Nazis marching with their equipment under the June sun to take up their positions on the nearby hills.

In Bominaco, the Germans have prepared artillery positions exactly around the well, and foxholes for infantry right behind the two ancient churches. I wonder what will happen in our area in the next few days? The Germans walk in long columns through the mountains to their defense line. Who knows what could happen to the group and to Lieutenant Ubaldo if they run into all these Nazi troops. We can only hope for the best! Lino didn't come, so I have no contact with them and I am sorry for that.

4 JUNE 1944

Giosi came running down and, almost choking from lack of breath, blurted out: "The Allies are in Rome! In Rome!" We embraced happily, but Mr. Giosi has another reason to be happy: yesterday he had a baby girl! So it's a double celebration! Lino arrived too, and told us that the Germans were unable to hold the area around Rome and were retreating. In our sector, the English have advanced too, but very slowly.

We have now been hidden at Antonio's brother's for eight days, but we don't think about the dangers hanging over us any more. We are cheerful because of the victories and hope to be liberated very soon. It's high time now.

5 JUNE 1944

The Germans have stopped all their fortification works and are getting ready for their defense. The British are getting nearer. We are nervous. We feel that all is not yet over for us. But we were told that now we are in the battle zone, we could risk fleeing. Lino brought us that information. Father and I have decided to leave for Bominaco tomorrow morning. I want to find out where the group is anyway. Lino will tell me where to go.

In the evening, we decided to hold a séance, just to pass the time and out of curiosity. For the first time in seven or eight months our moods were high. The "spirit" told us that Lino was the medium. Father used to take part in these sessions in his internment camps and, as usual, the questions were about "the situation." We asked the "spirit" when would we be liberated. The answer was: "In about two weeks." Hopefully he was right. Then we ask, among a host of other questions, the one big question that torments us all: "Will there be a second front in the west? And when?" The answer we received from the "spirit" was, "It is not necessary anymore!" We looked at each other, astounded. What did "he" mean "not necessary anymore?" A short time after midnight we went to sleep.

6 JUNE 1944

Early in the morning, we left the generous and hospitable

home of Natale Conte and, as the sun began to rise and
Allied airplanes "opened" the skies, we climbed the steep
road that leads to Bominaco. From time to time, we heard
the noise of thunder and explosions from the surrounding
mountains. Near the cemetery, halfway between Caporciano and Bominaco, we ran into a column of German
infantry marching slowly, cursing and swearing, in the
direction of their strongholds. But after a few meters we
managed to extricate ourselves from the column and take
a different path. The mountain in front of Bominaco — S.
Erasmo — now has a long colored pole at the top, a few
meters high. The Germans put it there, no doubt, as a
directional pole for their artillery.

We arrived in Bominaco, took Mother and Livio out of
their hiding place and went back to our old apartment. We
don't save bread anymore. I listened to the news on the
radio at Michele Agrippa's house: the Allies had landed
that morning in France! After a few more words, the radio
stopped transmitting: the Germans had blown up the
power station. It may have been the last item of news we
heard, but it sure was big news.

That same night, "Barbetta" also left the shelter of the
Aloisios' house and gathered what was left of his group,
dispersed for the last three weeks. Where can I find
Ubaldo's group?

We can hear explosions all around us. Ammunition
dumps are blowing up and on the fortified peak of S.
Erasmo we can see clouds of black smoke. How long will
it take now? The loss of electric power after the destruction
of the power plant doesn't bother us that much. At home,

184

since we were in Bominaco, we used a lantern anyway. And this evening, we "treated ourselves" to a very thick and plentiful lunch of chickpeas and lentils!

7 June 1944

The door opened and I suddenly saw Renato Osmo-Morris standing before me with his little dog Lilla, as well! The surprise left me speechless. Renato told us what had happened to them. The night they were arrested they were all taken to Sulmona, and then to a collecting camp near Pescara. Then, with the confusion of the battle raging all around, the Germans, so it seems, "lost their heads" and simply let them go. Renato covered 70 kilometers within 24 hours, moving between the lines and finally arriving here. He had not heard from Captain Alfred. We were very moved to see Renato. We decided to go to Opi in the afternoon.

We started walking along the narrow valley, accompanied by the noise of rumbling explosions echoing from one valley to the next. We didn't care very much about all that, for to our ears it was the sound of approaching freedom! We only worried about the lack of news now that the radio could not function anymore. While walking, I picked up a leaflet dropped behind the Germans lines. It said in German that the Allies had landed in Normandy. I took it with me.

We were welcomed in Opi with great joy, and taken to

the small woods where I was nearly brought to tears when I met the Russian and the four Englishmen once more after three weeks of perilous adventures. I told them the latest news. They were exultant with all the noise of battle surrounding us. It meant to them exactly what it meant to us. They also heard the story of the Osmo-Morris family's adventures.

The roads around us already showed the signs of war passing through the hills and mountains: empty cartridge cases from spent artillery shells; smoke here and there from nearby valleys; and from S. Demetrio, and everywhere around, signs of the retreating Germans — ammunition belts, rags, and even unit tags with rank and division number all tossed alongside the road. Renato wanted to leave in the morning and risk crossing no-man's land again. I found a copy of a travel order in a discarded Nazi office box on the road in Opi. I wrote a fake transit permit for Renato in German and signed it with the name "Sergeant Schulz." I stayed in Opi for the night.

As the sun set, my brother Livio arrived from Bominaco. He was quite hungry. He had had to cross the three-kilometer-long valley full of smoke to bring us the latest news. The British were in Popoli, about seven kilometers from Navelli as the crow flies. Then he left.

The next morning, Renato Osmo-Morris left on his dangerous trip attempting to cross no-man's land, armed with the fake German permit I had written, while I returned to Bominaco. War is something that seems quite paradoxical at times. One can see contrasting sights that are both scary and artistic. For instance, I sit with Father on the grass in a vineyard on the slope of a hill, under the hot sun; the air is shimmering from the heat. We are sweating, and the noise of flies and other insects fill the air. It seems odd that such a calm and beautiful scene can be broken by the sounds of war. Yet there we sit calmly on our hill as the blast of explosions and faraway rumbling of artillery tear the air around us. Against a beautiful blue sky, we see columns of smoke arising from the hill, and the German infantry marching on the path to Fontecchio. Until now the farmers haven't been very impressed by all this, and go about their work in the fields, checking their maturing wheat fields as they turn yellow.

9 JUNE 1944

I was sitting on the top of a hill higher than the castle below. With me was a dispatch rider from Ubaldo's group, a teacher by the name of Ascenzio Rosa — a young veteran of the Italian army in Russia. From our vantage point, we watched the operations of the German artillery with interest. Nazi guns were positioned below in Tussio, a little village near us, and were busy firing. Every thirty seconds, the air shook with an explosion, and down below we could see the flash of the gun barrels. What was fascinating was that far to the east along the road — about nine or ten kilometers from there — we could see the "impact point" of the German artillery shells as they fell: high "fountains" of earth that looked white from where we sat, rising and then slowly falling back to earth as shot after shot was fired. A German artillery gun was even posted inside Caporciano, near Antonio Conte's house.

The Degens' house (they had returned as well) was occupied by a whole German divisional headquarters, which had settled in with a general unit and signal unit.

Ascenzio and I could see a frightened red fox that had run away from a small cave on the side of the hill because of the racket. Poor animal. But I, for one, was happy.

We descended the hill. Near the first house in Bominaco we met a procession of wretched farmers. They were all crying and shouting, driving and pushing donkeys, sheep, cows and households in front of them. It looked like the end of the world.

What was happening?! They answered in unison that hundreds of retreating German soldiers were in Caporciano, plundering the village. They feared the same fate might befall Bominaco, so they were fleeing to the countryside.

Ascenzio Rosa went down to Caporciano and later told me what was happening there. The Germans were furious after the latest fighting. In their retreat they were plundering Caporciano — stealing horses, donkeys, carriages and food stocks. They had also arrested a score of men in the village. The orders for the 2nd company were to be ready for the coming days.

In the evening, while I was listening to conversations at Aloisios', a German car arrived in Bominaco. Nothing special. They were retreating and had taken a wrong turn, ending up in our hamlet. They were very scared and left quickly. From the plain, we could hear explosions. We went to bed.

11 JUNE 1944

The German retreat continues. German cavalry units are camped around Caporciano, leaving the horses to graze on the wheat fields, and making the farmers furious. What the horses don't eat, the Germans cut down with sickles taken from the farmers.

In the evening on the hill, from the side of the castle, we saw fires and explosions on the Caporciano plain. German demolition units crossed the area, followed by a huge explosion: the whole bottleneck of Civitaretenga was being blown up to block the Allied advance. The critical moment for us had arrived.

From that night, all that lay between Navelli and us was a wall of destruction, marked solely by German barbed wire and fortifications.

In the middle of the night I got an order to present myself to Lino in Caporciano in the early morning. The 2nd company had been given the command to attack.

We stayed awake with the Aloisios until late into the night. The farmers were calmer now, but they still hid their belongings. It is very strange how these farmers think to first save their donkeys and cows and only later worry about their wives and children…

12 JUNE 1944

I was in Caporciano early in the morning. First I went to Natale Conte's house. The inhabitants were still overwrought after the sacking of the village yesterday. The people feared the retreating German cover units still on the hills surrounding Caporciano, and even in the plain. From rumors brought by local farmers, it seemed that British units could already be seen in the Navelli plain yesterday evening, but I didn't know if this story was true. Who could check it out with all the confusion around us? We didn't have news from the radio, either. During the night, the German divisional headquarters that had quartered itself in Degen's house had evacuated, telling everybody that the Allies had landed at Venezia and Genova. I wonder if that's true? But the Germans guns are still in Tussio.

I reported to Lino, who was waiting for me at Antonio Conte's place. Where was Antonio at this point? Lino gave me two hand grenades, which I put in the pockets of my raincoat. I had to be ready. I understood that Lino and I would be some sort of "fifth column" inside Caporciano. I went to have lunch at Natale Conte's, with the hand grenades still stuffed in my pockets.

12 JUNE 1944, 2.30 P.M.

The 2nd company attacked Caporciano! The village was surrounded on three sides by my friends. One could hear rifle-fire from all sides. I ran out onto the terrace, grenades in hand, and surveyed the scene: I could see one of the partisans down below leaping forward, throwing himself on the ground and opening fire. I didn't know to where Lino had disappeared, but I surmised that it was too early to go out into the street. The sound of rifles and automatic weapons filled the air around us. I didn't know exactly what was happening. Natale's family was anxious and his daughters were very scared. I could hear quick bursts of sub-machine gun fire — the work of our homemade magazines, I guessed.

An explosion ripped the air: the Germans had blown up the field gun, about 60 meters from where I stood.

The attack proceeded, but the gunfire began to die down. Only here and there one could hear some automatic fire. I ran out to the road, gripping my two grenades. As I crossed the square of the town hall, I spotted the first partisans running in my direction, armed and excited. The first one I met was Serafino, the son of the fascist school teacher. Behind him, gripping a smoking sub-machine gun was Corrado — the crazy one. Antonio Conte followed, armed to the teeth with a rifle slung across his shoulders, a sub-machine gun in his hands, and ammunition and two revolvers stuck in his belt.

When we met, Serafino and I hugged each other. But there was no time to lose. I asked Antonio Conte what was up. His group had to ferret out the fascists, while Lieutenant Ubaldo and his men down below continued the attack. I could see how the partisans brought out some fascists, lined them up against a wall, but refrained from

191

shooting them. Among the prisoners, I could see secretary Taddeo Lino.

I ran down to the lower side of the village where there was still some firing going on. Somebody gave me a rifle, an ammo belt and three German hand grenades. The rifle was German as well. I didn't really know what I was doing, but I ran along following what the others did when I saw Ubaldo and his men running close to the houses for cover.

12 June 1944, 4 p.m.

Caporciano is ours! We are all hot, sweating and panting with the weapons heavy in our hands — dirty but free! Across the fields we saw Germans fleeing on a bicycle. They pedaled in the direction of the main road. Ubaldo sent some men to pursue them, but with little success.

Some very nice booty has fallen into our hands: a whole ammunition dump and some German hand grenades — some of which were defused by the Nazis at the last minute, but the majority are in working order. We also found some guns and rifles.

We climbed back up to the village. The 2nd company took over the house that only a short time earlier had been occupied by German soldiers. Now *we* were there. My brother, who had been in Caporciano all this time and was not scared off by the fighting, was horrified to see me with a gun on my shoulder and hand grenades dangling from my belt. But actually I had only 30 bullets and would have to save them carefully.

I saw Degen and his wife yelling on the steps. What was the matter? Mr. Degen was in such a fury that he didn't even see me. He was defending a fascist who had helped him and had now been arrested by the partisans. Ubaldo talked with Degen and explained to him that if the fascist really had done something good it would be discussed later on, but Degen refused to listen. The partisans refused to argue with them. They were furious. In the heat of the argument Mrs. Degen slipped, fell down the stairs and broke a leg. A very nice liberation!

We pulled the now-useless German field gun to the little square and placed it there as a "war trophy."

Meeting in a makeshift "operations room," Lieutenant Ubaldo spoke to us. We were now the masters in Caporciano and a squad was going to Bominaco to take control of the hamlet, too. But the whole situation was precarious and fluid: we had avoided trying to take any ground where the German cover forces were dug in, and we still didn't know exactly where the English were. Consequently, we would have to hold the villages until the Allies arrived. Those were our orders.

I finally found out Ubaldo's name and identity: his name is Ubaldo Nafissi and he is from Gubbio.

Gerald O'Shea walked down the street, cheerful and happy as a lark, enthralled to be free and among the partisans. He talked to everybody, without even noticing that nobody understood him!

193

I was exuberant, too. I was free — with a weapon in my hand! But I was also very dirty and very tired.

I was assigned to guard the fascists in the basement. There were about 30 prisoners, shaken and scared. The order was given to arrest even Professor Servetto, who had given us the house in Bominaco, but he had escaped and so his wife was taken instead. I was very sorry for that, but I couldn't do anything to counter my orders. In the evening, a partisan escorted my brother back to Bominaco so that he would not have to walk the three kilometers alone. After a two-hour shift, somebody relieved me on guard duty. I took a little rest, but it was very difficult with the ceaseless bustle of boots and noise of weapons.

12 JUNE 1944, 9 P.M.

Ubaldo received news that some 2,000 enemy troops covering the German's retreat may be planning to cross our sector as they left via the Civitaretenga bottleneck.

Again, another meeting was convened. The orders called for the 2nd company to cross the plain by night and cut off the main street near the road inspector's house. Our leader was to be Antonio Conte. Ubaldo and part of the company remained in Caporciano. Under cover of dark, we mined the two roads leading to Caporciano with our shell-mines. I was in the squad under Antonio's direct command as we moved out marching single file, following a little side road. The German defensive line in Civitaretenga was silent. On the way to our objective we found ourselves facing a small minefield. The men in the advanced scout unit had discovered it. Antonio Conte decided to disarm the mines, taking me and another man with him. I was quite scared. Antonio gave me a lit candle. While I held the candle, trembling with fear, he defused the mines — totally calm. Crazy. There were four mines and nothing happened. Then we proceeded on our way.

12 JUNE 1944, 11 P.M.

We reached our objective and took up our positions, cutting the main road. Antonio left some men to cover us from the wheat field, while we trampled the asphalt of the road with our hobnailed boots, in preparation to camouflage our shell-mines, should we have to lay them. Antonio fired three rockets to signal Caporciano that we had reached our objective, but nobody answered.

The night was silent and full of stars. A mere two miles to our north, between Tussio and S. Pio, there were six German field guns that had been active during the last few days. But tonight all was quiet.

We settled down in the inspector's half-destroyed house. Scattered around us were the burned remains of German cars. I and another three stood guard throughout the night.

The hours passed very slowly as we lay down near the

windows, cradling our weapons, jumpy and nervous, but with heavy eyes.

We jumped as six explosions broke the silent night. We learned the reason a half-hour later when a courier arrived: the Germans had blown up the six guns not far from our position. What about the retreating German cover forces? They had moved out very slowly, in front of us. Nobody knew what would happen. I slept for about an hour.

At about 4:30 in the morning, the stars slowly disappeared as the first signs of dawn appeared on the horizon.

13 June 1944

It was to be a very hot day. Already at six in the morning a strong sun had begun to smother the countryside with its warmth. Antonio Conte sent for new orders from Caporciano, and we got our reply: we were to patrol the area up to the German barbed wire at Civitaretenga. Antonio himself went out, taking me and a one-eyed partisan — whose brother had been deported by the Germans — with him. I agreed, as tired as I was.

We walked very slowly and warily along the ditch paralleling the main road. It was very hot. From time to time we stopped in the middle of the wheat field to look around us. All was silent.

After an hour of scouting we reached a point not far from the destroyed narrow pass. From our position we saw a huge heap of rubble, stones and earth. The German barbed wire parameter fence was clearly visible on the rocks. The noise of explosions continued on the other side of the plain of Navelli, four kilometers behind the Civitaretenga bottleneck.

Towards evening we were alerted by the messenger Ubaldo (who had been with us since noon) that German forces might try to cross the main road we were holding. Alarmed, we hastily laid our shell-mines along the road and dug in between two rows of mines. A cover line held the way open for us to retreat to Caporciano and mountains, come what might. We were all very tense. My exhaustion dissipated under the stress. Nobody was to pass: these were our orders.

The tense silence was broken by a tremendous explosion! To the north, about two kilometers from our position, we saw the electric power plant slowly rising into the air, then disintegrating in a cloud of dust — spelling the end of the S. Pio power station! The Germans had thus effectively blocked the main road.

Nighttime descended upon us — our second night on alert at the front line. Nobody slept. To the north of our positions, we heard a whole succession of explosions that went on all night long, painting the sky with a red-blue light. At midnight, we heard that units of the adjacent group under Captain Giovanni Aloisi had taken up positions between S. Pio and Castelnuovo, but had not reached the main road. They lay in the fields and olive groves bordering the road.

That night, too, ended without incident, but alert

conditions remained in force. We tested our weapons and noted that they functioned well.

14 June 1944

The morning was stifling hot and filled with incidents. We were blocking the main road, but there was not an enemy in sight. The farmers didn't care about the war. They had come down to work in their fields. My eyes were red and swollen after two sleepless nights. The tension and fatigue of marching in the hot weather had been exhausting. Antonio Conte decided that I and ten other men would return to the barracks in Caporciano for 24 hours of rest. We were to withdraw with our arms and leave in the afternoon.

Suddenly there was an alert! Somebody was approaching down the road on a motorcycle! In the midst of a cloud of dust we could only see the glitter of weapons. When they came into sight we loosened our fingers on the trigger; they were two partisan officers of the "Gran Sasso" brigade, come to inspect the various units. News? The retreating German cover forces had broken through a sector of the brigade, opening the way to the north. It seemed that our area was still not in the way of the Nazis.

Another man on a motorcycle arrived: a *carabiniere* on duty with the brigade. Since I was chosen to escort him to headquarters, I took advantage of his vehicle and he took me to Caporciano instead of walking the long, hot four kilometers of road and uphill paths.

After sleeping for some hours, which only made my swollen eyes hurt all the more, I commenced my duty at the command post. Ubaldo told me that while we were making out way to block the main road, my father had come to visit him and told him what that fascist Taddeo Lino had done for us and how he had helped us, thus convincing Ubaldo to let him go. So now Lino is free.

In the evening, when it was not so hot, Father and Livio finally came to see me after many days apart. They live in Bominaco, and were still feeling very insecure between the noise of the explosions and the sense that full liberation was still far away. He warned me, "Only when the British arrive and advance even further northward will we really be free. Your partisans could be swept away by the Germans in less than an hour." Of course, my father was not totally off the mark in his evaluation. Just then, Mr. Giosi passed by, singing and whistling, absent-mindedly as usual, nothing other than *Giovinezza* — an old fascist hymn! An angry partisan stopped him and could have shot him on the spot had my father not held him back. In the end, all three had a laugh about it!

Instead of 24 hours rest, I had to go back the same evening to the position we were manning on the main road, but in another place. This time, I was posted near the little shack, together with Serafino and Riccardo, and armed with automatic weapons. The whole company had been put on alert again, because German infantry and mountain-troops have been spotted on the move in the mountains. The order remained the same: nobody was allowed pass through. We spent a third night stretched out in the fields, cradling our weapons.

15 JUNE 1944

The tension has eased. During the night the German units abandoned their positions and chose to bypass us, preferring to retreat via the mountain roads than try to break through via the main highway, blocked by our partisan groups.

Now we are practically in no-man's land, between two battling forces. We lay all day long on the two sides of the road. Even so, we sweat, perhaps because our skin is so coated with dirt. Tonight I can finally sleep at last, as long as the stars are out.

16 JUNE 1944

It is a funny feeling to find oneself in a no-man's land, even if we have the 2nd partisan company with us. But one can never know what will happen in such a power vacuum, caught between two firing lines. The British are to our south and the Germans to our north, waging war against each other while our orders remain the same. We are to permit Allied forces to pass through, but open fire on anybody else.

A platoon of partisans from the Majella brigade has arrived across the mountains to reinforce our positions. They are serving as scouts for advancing British forces. The British should be about three kilometers from us. These boys of the Majella look dangerous and savage, and truly they are armed to the teeth, loaded with weapons and ammunition belts to boot. They supply themselves with hand grenades from our captured ammo dump.

16 JUNE 1944, 1 P.M.

I was given an order to scout to our south — unescorted! I received an old shaky bicycle for my mission, and must have looked rather funny donned in a pair of half-torn khaki shorts, a blue open skirt wrapped around my head like a pirate's handkerchief as protection from the sun, a loaded rifle across my shoulders, a haversack with some food and spare underpants, an ammo belt and the three German hand grenades at my side.

Slowly I proceeded down the road. All was quiet and the air was hot. The silence was unnerving after the last ten days of commotion.

I arrived below Civitaretenga. It was difficult to cross the narrow bottleneck: there was tangled German barbed wire everywhere. The houses on the side of the road had been reduced to heaps of rubble. The road itself was chaotic — filled with holes, rubble and stones. The destroyed mill and everything else was wrapped in a cloud of dust and there was the danger of land mines everywhere. To negotiate the mines as safely as possible, I decided to follow the footprints left by the German demolition troops and farmers that could be clearly discerned in the dust. If they crossed without being blown up, so could I. I gingerly negotiated these two hundred meters of treacherous turf, proceeding slowly through the ruins as if I were walking on eggs; only these eggs were lethal.

16 June 1944, 2.30 p.m.

As I proceeded down the road into the Navelli plain, the surroundings were shaken suddenly by sharp explosions. I was quite scared, because from time to time I could see flashes and fountains of earth being blown into the sky by incoming artillery shells in the fields on my left. Suddenly I stopped dead in my tracks: before me on the road were people with helmets glittering in the sun, dressed in khaki uniforms and short trousers. The British!

I jumped on my bicycle and flew across the last hundred meters, almost falling onto two British officers who were surveying the area. I was exhilarated! I was among the liberating soldiers!

The two British officers checked me over from head to foot and, realizing I was a partisan, began questioning me about the situation beyond the narrow bottleneck. I told them all I knew and added that 11 kilometers from where we stood — in Opi — there were escaped British prisoners in a sector only partially controlled by the partisans. I continued on with the British scouts. The air there felt better.

Helmeted British soldiers were everywhere, resting along the road. In the fields, other British soldiers with magnetic mine detectors were sweeping the area for mines. The Germans had laid a field of about 4,000 mines in Navelli!

I got closer to the village. Near the road-inspection house, among the scene of mass destruction, bomb craters and a thick cloud of dust, hundreds of men from Navelli were working under the direction of the British to fill in bomb craters with earth and stones. Many of them greeted me happily.

A line of dusty camouflaged British vehicles was parked under the chestnut trees near the house, and soldiers were resting in the shade. I was quite impressed to see the British scouting units in Navelli. Navelli was being occupied by the British — the same Navelli we left four months earlier, hunted like wild beasts!

I climbed up to the town council house and was stunned to meet Aurelio, Ugo...and Umberto, who had been nominated town mayor by the British military administration. They had escaped from the convoy of trucks deporting them to Germany after being captured and, with great difficulty, had managed to return to Navelli. Now they wore an armband with the national colors and the letters C.L.N. We were terribly happy to meet again.

Together with Bruno the communist, I went to the house where Cannata the spy lived. I entered with my rifle, ready to fire. His wife yelled that they were innocent. Her husband, the painter, had escaped to a safer place. I was furious and ready to shoot the wife for being a spy as well, but Bruno grabbed me and dragged me away.

After staying for over two hours in British-held territory, I had to go back into no-man's land to my position with my partisan comrades. While I was returning along the forward British positions, a sharp explosion ripped the air. A British soldier had stepped on a mine. I could see his comrades carry the half-dead victim away, wounded and bleeding.

I returned the same way I had come, and within an hour was back again with the 2nd company. Joyfully, I reported that the Allies were now near Civitaretenga, but I didn't know when they would start their advance again. Antonio Conte sent me to Caporciano, where I reported to Ubaldo about the British already being in Navelli. There were no Germans around us for a radius of at least six or seven kilometers, and all was quiet.

I got a very short leave. I went to Natale Conte's and found my family and the Aloisio family there, so I could tell them about the English soldiers already in Navelli. Mother was frightened to see me going about with all the weapons, but I only laughed.

I remained all night in Caporciano, on duty at the command post. The fascist prisoners were still in the cellar, but Lieutenant Ubaldo called them to him, one by one. Since I was present, I could hear what he said. He explained the situation to them, saying he had no intention of putting them on trial. That was the prerogative of the law, but he was under orders to keep them under arrest until the whole area was completely liberated.

All in all, the fascists fare quite well: they get their food from their families and only complain about the suffocating heat in the cellar, crammed in as they are, 50 or 60 of them all together.

With the dawn of a new day, I returned with fresh men to man our positions, but knowing that the Allies were a mere three kilometers distance from us made us much calmer. In the event anything should go wrong for us, we could always retreat to their positions. But we now waited impatiently for them to take over our area.

.

17 JUNE 1944

Our duty along the road is boring and tiresome. We can hear the noise of gunfire and explosions from somewhere, but it is not very clear from where. In any case, we are too tired to try and figure it out and don't care very much. It is very hot. We put our guns in the shade under the bushes, because after a long time exposed to the hot sun, the gun barrels get so hot they burn our skin.

Somewhere a German soldier was captured. Where and how we don't know. At last they brought him to the road, with his hands up. He was very pale and scared. I served as interpreter. He belonged to the German units that were laying mines to cover the retreat of the German troops, that had later scattered. He was trembling. We decided to use him to clear out some minefields already discovered but not completely cleared. He walked with our rifles at his back, and showed us the mines left or put down by his group. He was scared and believed we wanted to kill him.

After he finished his "mission," I spoke with this unlucky fellow in German. He claimed he was not a Nazi — that it was not his business. He was from Thüringen. I asked him where the Germans to our north were located. He either didn't know or didn't want to tell me. For the last few days, he claimed, he had been completely lost in the confusion of the retreat. He looked like a rag. After another hour we got the command to free the German. We didn't know what to do with him. He was given a civilian jacket and, much to his great surprise, a kick in the ass. We let him go on the road, under the broiling sun.

In the afternoon, an Allied patrol arrived with much commotion, stopping briefly at our position, and then moved on. After half an hour they were back in a big cloud of dust. They had crossed the "unmanned" area three to four kilometers to the north of our last sentries, then returned. We couldn't fathom why the British had stopped here, just under our noses.

18 JUNE 1944

Duty on the main road again. Everything is as silent as a grave, with the sun burning down. Early in the morning, a British armored patrol crossed our positions on a scouting mission, but quickly returned. We were exhausted from six days on alert, guarding the road from the ditches but not doing anything special. Ubaldo said that those were our orders.

We saw someone walking alone on the road. But it was no one special, only a prostitute freed from a German prison. I didn't know what she was doing there, but in any case, Ascenzio Rosa and Riccardo availed themselves of her services and then, cursing, let her proceed in the direction of the British lines.

In the afternoon I was at our headquarters in Caporciano. I met my brother, who had come with the former prisoners from Opi and Afanacio the Russian. They were all very happy. We greeted one another, and the partisans welcomed them all with joy.

Then I got the directive — something I would have done willingly without an order — to take them to the British lines. We left a short time later, escorted for a while by partisans. We walked, talking happily. Gerald O'Shea went with us as well. He decided to follow us to the Allied lines. We passed Navelli after an hour on the road. It was very moving to see the first meeting of my British friends with a British unit in a jeep on an exploratory mission. They ran towards the vehicle and almost choked the two soldiers in it with their hugs. The pair gave us some information about the war. For the last two weeks, we'd known almost nothing. The Allies were advancing in France, nearing Firenze and Ancona. We stopped at Navelli for a short time. The British and I stayed at the office of the C.L.N. Toward evening, we moved on.

20 JUNE 1944

For the last two days I have been in Allied territory. I returned this evening, very tired.

We left Navelli for Popoli, about 15 kilometers further on, parallel to the British positions. Once more, we entered a kind of no-man's land, held by the Majella partisans. In Popoli, we slept in an empty barrack. The next day, we watched the British armored units enter the city. I had a hard time recognizing the town at all. Everything was bombed out and in ruins. All the areas we had crossed in the last few days had been damaged considerably by the latest fighting. Near Sulmona, I finally turned over all the former British POWs to a British patrol, and returned to Popoli with Afanacio. Then we marched to Bussi, where British army engineers were building a bridge to replace the old one blown up by the Germans. We crossed the river on a temporary bridge built by the partisans, and found ourselves again in no-man's land. I was now quite fed up and started cursing when I met up once more with a British-partisan mixed patrol. I turned the Russian over to them. Our parting was very emotional; Afanacio was almost crying.

Now I had to cover 22 kilometers from east to west. I walked the distance unescorted in one day under a burning sun, moving parallel to the Allied forward positions, following a pretty bad road. In the evening, I reached the Civitaretenga bottleneck. Leaving the British advanced units, I entered the "unoccupied" area we held between the two sides again. Lieutenant Ubaldo sent me at once to Bominaco to my family, who were worried because of my absence.

I spent a few nice and cheerful hours in Bominaco. With the Allies but a short distance away, my family was feeling better, and eating bigger slices of bread, even bigger quantities of chickpeas! Everybody else felt good, too. Everyone was in high spirits.

At night, I went back to my position. My comrades welcomed me cheerfully. A patrol of British soldiers and Italian paratroopers from the "Nembo" division stayed with us throughout a foggy night. I slept in a ditch like a stone, cradling my rifle, lucky not to have drawn guard duty.

21 JUNE 1944

The day started with a burning sun and quickly got only hotter. The Germans were now completely out of our area. Wherever we patrolled the nearby roads, we saw wrecks of the former German war machine — some six or seven abandoned cannons, and entire dumps of artillery shells abandoned in the retreat. Things seemed to be in complete chaos. Again, we couldn't understand why the British had stopped where they had, without taking over the entire area, including what we partisans were now holding.

We were informed that the main body of the "Gran Sasso" brigade with elements of the "Majella" brigade had occupied Aquila without waiting for the British advance. They had discovered a grave with nine bodies of partisans, shot by the Germans, in the potato field next to the "National Sharpshooters House" I had once visited with Heinz.

We were completely fed up doing nothing in no-man's land, but it seemed that these were our orders. Then suddenly in the first hours of the afternoon, without warning, a British armored force from Civitaretenga began to advance in a cloud of dust in our direction. The main British and Italian force followed. In a whirlwind, the column of the Allied war machines passed by our cheering groups of partisans, heading north after the retreating Germans.

FINALLY, WE ARE FREE!

Going Home

Now we were free. No more fear of sudden searches by the Germans, no more dread of deportation to "somewhere" sinister and unknown. We were just normal, free people.

I received my "demobilization" orders, handed over my rifle, two hand grenades and ammunition, and returned to "civilian" life with my family in Bominaco. We could not return to Fiume.

The main problem now was finding a home and some kind of employment. In the middle of July, my father finally made some contacts, and managed to obtain some work through the Union of Jewish Communities in Italy. He was sent as cantor, teacher and coordinator on Jewish community business to a Displaced Persons (D.P.) camp in Santa Croce, near Lecce, in southern of Italy. The camp was administrated by the recently created UNRA, an agency that took care of the organization and relief of the mounting numbers of refugees in Europe (mainly Jews). We stayed there until the end of the war.

My father went a couple of times to Rome to inquire about possible work and finding a place to live. At last, he came across Mr. Feyer, an old friend from his early days as an "interned person" in 1940. Mr. Feyer promised Father some kind of work with the Jewish community in Milano, as well as the temporary use of his apartment, in which he had lived before the war. So, we started to prepare for the move to Milano.

In October we arrived in Milano. We were taken to the provisional Jewish community center, now partly used as a transit point for refugees.

Father started to work within the Jewish community, while my brother and I finally began to attend a normal school.

Through the help of a young *Hechalutz* ("Pioneer") youth group member, my friend Guido and I found our so long sought-after contact with the Jews in Palestine. I had become increasingly focused on what was happening there. Somebody belonging to the *Hagana* — the Jewish defense organization in Jewish Palestine — began to inform us daily of events in *Eretz Yisrael*.

The fighting was spreading, and the news was not always good.

In order to leave Italy, we were once again new and different identities, mainly because we were to travel on a "legal" ship. I received a Dutch passport bearing my own name and photograph, but I was never able to remember the name of my supposed place of birth. The remarkable item in this passport was an entry visa, again with my name, signed by the British High Commissioner of Palestine. I am sure it was a forgery. Some of us even received cheap suitcases for our belongings, so we would look somewhat like tourists, though I cannot believe that anybody really wishing to inspect this "tourist group" would have believed we were legitimate travelers.

So, passing as a Dutch tourist, I set sail for the "Promised Land" on board the *Kedma*. With first light of the sixth day, we saw the shore. It was hardly dramatic: just low, bare hills, and one bigger hill– almost a mountain — with a small, plain town of white houses surrounding it. That was the Carmel Mountain and the northern town of Haifa. We all came up on deck to have a look. I don't remember what I was thinking at that moment, but I know I was impressed by the very *lack* of any special scenery. The ship approached the port, but did not enter. The harbor was choked with British ships, navy and merchant vessels. England was evacuating her huge army, and we "illegals" were not permitted to disembark.

Some naval administrative business (I don't know what exactly) was conducted with our ship, the *Kedma*, and towards evening we took off again, this time slowly following the shoreline north. Then we stopped, and I noticed some light signals coming from the land. We were called up on deck, organized in groups of about a hundred and told to wait. The sea was not very calm, and fast waves were running in the direction of the beach. Suddenly we heard some engine noises, and a motor boat appeared on the dark sea dragging a large wooden raft behind it, and then another one. Group by group we climbed down the sides of the ship and onto the rafts. The rafts were dancing heavily on the waves, so we sat down and were dragged to the beach, some hundred yards away. At one point the cable snapped, and we were left drifting around about until someone from the motor boat managed to jump onto our raft and tie it up to the boat again.

At last we jumped onto the beach, where we were collected by armed *Hagana* soldiers and taken to a group of busses waiting on the nearby road. We were somewhere between the Jewish village of Nahariya and the recently occupied Arab town of Akko, better known to us by its historical name of Saint John of Acre.

We were taken to a camp somewhere near Kiryat Motzkin—or maybe it was Kiryat Biyalik, I don't remember—close to the refineries, and welcomed by the Jewish military authorities.

WE WERE HOME AT LAST!

Epilogue

By **Noga Fleischmann**

After the Mahal volunteers disembarked they were taken
to the Technion in Haifa, where they underwent superficial
checks, gave a short medical history, were classified and
then sent off on brief exercises. Luigi became a machine
gunner and, until the fighting died down in 1949, fought
on various fronts — in the Jezreel Valley, against the
Iraqis, on the southern front, in the Beer Tuvia area, in
Ashkelon, in Beersheba, and even in Eilat (then called Um
Rashrash).

In August 1949, Luigi was offered demobilization. He
bid farewell to his fellow soldiers and was discharged
from service. For a while he stayed with his uncle in Tel
Aviv and worked in a garage. Then he decided to return
to Italy in order to learn a useful trade for his future life
in Isracl. He had no doubt whatsoever: this was what
he wanted — to be in *Eretz Yisrael*. Having entered the
country illegally, as a volunteer, he contacted the Italian

consulate in Jerusalem in order to get a *laissez-passer* for Italy. He was given a very chilly reception. He was advised to return to Italy the way he had left — in other words, illegally. So Luigi stayed for a short time with his friend and comrade-in-arms David Cohen, whose family had adopted him and given him a home while he was in Israel. At the end of December 1949, he left for Italy.

After five days at sea, Luigi reached the port of Genoa. When he disembarked and presented his papers, the passport officer politely asked Luigi to accompany him to an inner room. After the door closed behind him, he realized he was under arrest. He was not allowed to call his family in Milano, so they remained unaware of his situation. The upshot was that Luigi spent about a month in the "cooler," until one of the prisoners who was about to be released agreed to memorize the phone number of the Fleishmann family. He called them and told them that their son was in jail. Some three weeks later, Luigi's brother arrived from Milano with the requisite paperwork. Luigi's belt, watch and shoelaces were returned to him, and he set off for home. One can only imagine the joy of his parents at their son's safe return from the war.

It was now time to decide what he would learn that would be of benefit in Israel. Luigi decided to take a course in operating agricultural machinery. He was the only Jewish student. In March 1951, he left Milano once again for Israel, this time with a completely legal passport, but heading for an unknown future.

When he arrived in Israel, Luigi went back to stay with David Cohen and his family. David's sister Nira and her husband proposed that he join them working with field crops at Hadassim, a boarding school in the Sharon area, where we met. I was a student at the school and fell in love with him immediately. We married a year later, and stayed at Hadassim for about another a year. Then we went south, to the moshav of Kfar Warburg. There Luigi operated and maintained the moshav's water pumps, a job he continued to perform until retiring in January 1994. Our two daughters, Liora and Elisheva, whom he loved to distraction, were born in Kfar Warburg. He told each of them wonderful tales and drew unique figures. Luigi spent all his spare time reading and drawing. He had an inexhaustible store of knowledge about every subject under the sun, but his main love was history. In his drawings, he documented the wars in which he had taken part, always emphasizing their human aspect. After the Six Day War, he spent whole nights painting an entire epic, a major work documenting the war for future generations. It was his caring side that during the war took him to Khan Yunis where, together with the man responsible for local water supplies, he volunteered to fix the system for the the residents. That is how Luigi was, and that is how he should be remembered: a caring person, somebody who loved people and was loved by all –his family, his children and grandchildren, his neighbors, his colleagues and his friends.

Luigi died of cancer on August 23, 1999.

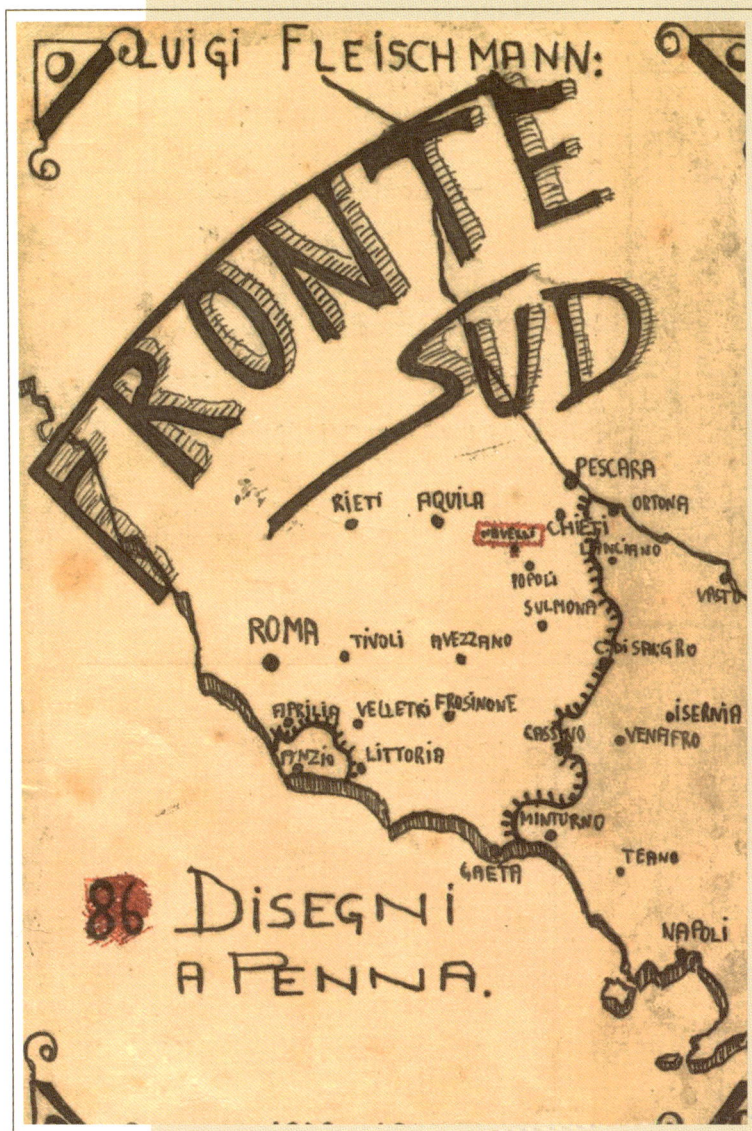

Map of area sketched by Luigi.

German tanks under
the snow, in front of the
Fleischmanns' home.

Only three steps away from a
German light gun vomiting fire,
and the artillerymen are like
stones, fearless.

4 or 5 planes attacking
a German convoy.

Tank in movement,
with Navelli in the background.

Opposite:
The castle on top of the hill,
Bominaco.

R. Heidmann
1944
Raminon

K. Kirchmann
1944
Banninard

Bominaco.

Opposite: Bominaco, 1944.

The destroyed plane and
the English pilot laying next
to it.

The plane of the English pilot
shot down by the Germans.

German soldiers in Navelli.

German soldiers in Navelli.

Navelli, sketch of town square, 1944.

Town square of Navelli.

View and town square of Navelli.

The Germans are parking their motor vehicles
and trucks, and unloading the cases.

View of Navelli.

Italian partisan certificate
given to Luigi.

RAGGRUPPAMENTO PATRIOTI "GRAN SASSO"

SEZIONE L'AQUILA

N. 115/A/8 di Prot.   L'Aquila, 24 settembre 1944

OGGETTO: Certificato.

      Si certifica che Il Partigiano FLEISMANN LUIGI di Giulio, nato a
Fiume il 17 aprile 1928, ha fatto parte della Banda " Giovanni Di Vin-
cenzo, Gruppo Caporciano?

      Si rilascia il presente in attesa del tesserino.

                        IL COMANDANTE DELLA BANDA "G. DI VINCENZO"
                          (Sottotenente Giovanni Ricottilli)

Steps in Navelli.

Family photo in DP camp,
from left to right: Luigi,
Luigi's mother and father
(josephina and Julio) and
brother Livio.

The municipality building, Navelli.

Noga and Luigi,
Eilat, 1996

Elisheva and Luigi,
Tiberias, 1998.

Liora and Luigi,
Tiberias, 1998.

Luigi and Noga,
Tiberias, 1998.

From left to right:
Liora, Luigi, Elisheva and Noga,
Kfar Warburg, 1999.

Celebration of Luigi's 70th birthday
with Noga, Tiberias, 1998.

Elisheva and Luigi at home,
Kfar Warburg.

Luigi, Tiberias, 1998.